NOT
IN MY
CLASSROOM

NOT IN MY CLASSROOM

A TEACHER'S GUIDE TO EFFECTIVE CLASSROOM MANAGEMENT

Frederick C. Wootan
and
Catherine H. Mulligan, M.A.

Adams Media
Avon, Massachusetts

To my wonderful wife, Barbara, who patiently cleans and cooks and waits for me to finish grading papers or making up tests, or writing, so we may spend a few minutes of together time each evening. To all those dedicated teachers who really work hard at their profession, and do so for the love of the children.

❧

Published by
Adams Media, an F+W Publications Company
57 Littlefield Street, Avon, MA 02322 U.S.A.
www.adamsmedia.com

ISBN 10: 1-59869-342-5
ISBN 13: 978-1-59869-342-3

Printed in Canada.

J I H G F E D C

Library of Congress Cataloging-in-Publication Data
Wootan, Fred C.
Not in my classroom / Frederick C. Wootan ;
with a technical review by Catherine H. Mulligan.
p. cm.
ISBN-13: 978-1-59869-342-3 (pbk.)
ISBN-10: 1-59869-342-5 (pbk.)
1. Classroom management. I. Title.
LB3013.W68 2007
371.102'4—dc22
2007001128

This publication is designed to provide accurate and authoritative information with regard to the subject matter covered. It is sold with the understanding that the publisher is not engaged in rendering legal, accounting, or other professional advice. If legal advice or other expert assistance is required, the services of a competent professional person should be sought.
—From a *Declaration of Principles* jointly adopted by a Committee of the American Bar Association and a Committee of Publishers and Associations

Many of the designations used by manufacturers and sellers to distinguish their product are claimed as trademarks. Where those designations appear in this book and Adams Media was aware of a trademark claim, the designations have been printed with initial capital letters.

Interior images © Stockbyte

This book is available at quantity discounts for bulk purchases.
For information, please call 1-800-289-0963.

Contents

Acknowledgments

I have always taken to heart my late college history professor's comment: "A little knowledge is a dangerous thing. Drink deep or taste not at all." I spent thirty-plus years in the insurance industry and studied it in depth, focused on it daily, and taught its concepts to both newcomers and practitioners for many years.

Once I made the leap into education full-time I did the same thing. I attended seminars. I asked questions of fellow teachers. I listened to teachers' conversations everywhere I went. I spent my summers traveling to locations important to the subject matter of my teaching to add depth to my lectures.

I could never have done these things so successfully without the full cooperation and love of Barbara, my wife of more than forty years. She ensconced herself in her careers of wife, mother, housewife, lover, and our family health practitioner. She always wanted to be involved in the medical field but put aside that ambition to become really good at all those other family jobs. Our house has been the repository for books on medications, remedies, child psychology, husband-wife relationships, and any educational type of television program dealing with interpersonal relationships. A self-taught woman, she taught me all my male brain could absorb and loved me whether or not I "got it." Without her keeping my head on straight with her abundance of common sense, I am not sure where I would have wandered.

I would be remiss if I didn't recognize the importance of genetics and childhood home life in my development. I thank my loving mother for her firm, never-wavering focus on the importance of family, love, and God. I thank my father for demonstrating without complaint the work ethic needed to keep his family fed and clothed. I believe I inherited his happy and friendly disposition toward all people, thereby opening many doors to information I would otherwise never have had the privilege of receiving.

Several years ago I suffered a serious financial disaster in my business and felt I had let my family down. That is, until my brother told me he would always look up to and respect me in addition to loving me as his big brother. My sister, like my brother, never wavered in her faith in me as a good person; a person she is proud to call her brother. I thank and love you both for that.

My son, Michael, and daughter, Abigail, have never given me pause to wonder if they loved or respected me. They have always made me feel that I'm the best father anyone could have. How could a father ask for or expect more?

For most of my adult life I have had the honor of having two very close friends who just happen to be educators. Donna and Denny Noggle probably didn't realize I was picking their brains all those years because they were so willing to share their knowledge. They have been dedicated to teaching kids up to age eighteen for their entire working careers. Even now, in their retirement, they are working with state department of education officials to help assure the people of our state that the job of teaching their children is being accomplished in the most professional and safest manner possible. You two deserve medals for your contributions to society.

Just recently the man who hired me at Fenwick High School died in a tragic automobile accident. He was a beacon of success in this field because of his devotion to the kids.

There were more than six thousand people at his funeral as a testament to the greatness of this man. Father Chuck Mentrup, I thank you for having faith in me, and for showing so many kids how to live, and how to love.

When Father Chuck received my letter asking about a teaching position, he passed it along to then Dean of Academics Mrs. Catherine Mulligan. Cathi, a true student of the process of education and a lover of kids, called me. The first thing she said was that she had recently discovered my novels in the school library and was reading one of them. She wanted an English teacher to focus on writing skills and was excited to discuss it with me. Cathi, you have retained that excitement not only for me and what I am doing with the students, but for our school and the kids. You deserve the job of principal that you accepted last year, and I enjoy working for such an intelligent and supportive person.

A big thanks to all the wonderful teachers at Fenwick High School. You all willingly share your teaching knowledge and experience as well as your daily classroom experiences, allowing me to grow exponentially in my teaching experience.

A writer must always have someone read what he or she produces or the rough drafts will remain just that—rough. Over the years I have come to rely on my sister-in-law, Mary Jo Milillo. Mary Jo, you actually seem to enjoy reading my manuscripts and also telling it like it is. Thank you for your willing help.

My brother-in-law, Ed Lampton, has been an inspiration by the mere fact that he reads voraciously and manages somehow to retain it. Our discussions are probably the closest thing to invigorating intellectual games I have ever experienced. Ed, I thank you for being a lifelong friend, confidant, and the guy I can always count on for help wherever I might need it.

A writer operating in a vacuum is not doing anything for his or her fellow man. If I had anything worthwhile to say on the subject of managing my classroom it had to be said in a concise, focused manner; follow a logical sequence; and be pleasurable to read. I would never have accomplished all those things without help, a depth of interest, and a challenge to improve my work. I thank you, Paula Munier and Brendan O'Neill, my editors.

I also want to thank all the students, both those in the insurance field and those here at Fenwick whom I have had the honor to teach. You have all taught me more than you will ever know. I have told you all this in person and I want to say it here. Every person has to work at something throughout his or her life; it is the especially fortunate who get to do something they love. Teaching is it for me. I love my students and there is no place on earth I would rather be than here in this classroom with you.

Foreword *by Catherine H. Mulligan, M.A.*

As I write this foreword, it is August and a new school year is about to start. In my career as teacher/administrator for more than forty years, I have often observed that at this time of year, successful teachers experience a renewal of enthusiasm for the role we play in facilitating learning. Although the end of a year in May or June is always welcome, so also is the start of a fresh year. Some regard this as irony; I regard it as a miracle. The "miracle" of renewed enthusiasm happens because we feel a sense of efficacy: what we do as teachers makes a difference in students' learning. *Student success depends very much on what takes place between teachers and students in the classroom.*

Boredom, disorganization, dead time, inappropriate student interaction, whining, acting out, irresponsibility, cheating, defiance, inattention . . . any teacher can make a list of classroom issues that diminish the effectiveness of our efforts to engage students in learning in our classrooms. Regarding each of these, we declare, "NOT IN *MY* CLASSROOM!"

Not in My Classroom is a resource for teachers who believe that a proactive approach to classroom management paves the way for class time to be truly valuable. By setting expectations for behavior and routine at the beginning of the year, and consistently adhering to these, the teacher creates an environment where learning, rather than attention to distraction, is always the focus. This book's "voice" is that of a practicing teacher, effectively supplementing ideas found in more formal settings such as teacher education courses or professional journals.

Fred Wootan brings a fresh perspective to classroom management. After a career as an executive in the insurance industry, with writing mystery novels and training manuals as a sideline, he joined the ranks of classroom teachers in 2003. One day (when coincidentally, I had perused one of his novels in our library), I received an inquiry from Fred, an alumnus of our school, about the possibility of teaching. A subsequent conversation confirmed his knowledge of writing and literature, but left a void concerning his classroom skills. Prior to his first day of teaching American literature in August of that year, his experience of the high school classroom had been as a student several decades previous. Would he experience culture shock? Déjà vu? Would he wonder, "What have I gotten myself into?" I'm not sure whether he had any of these thoughts, but I do know that he had that sense of efficacy, believing that his instructional practices, knowledge, and rapport with students could have a positive effect on student achievement.

In this book, Fred details the practices that have contributed to his personal success as a classroom teacher. He recognizes that relationships between students and teacher are very important, just as between businessman and client. Building the relationship begins in knowing students' names, progresses to knowing the students, and culminates in trust. A relationship built on respect, consistency, and trust enables a teacher to issue challenges that students will accept.

In the business world, quality control is essential. Businesspeople are trained to assess production, make changes based on data, and evaluate whether a change made a significant difference in productivity. Similarly, the successful teacher makes time for reflection, or taking stock of his or her classroom performance. A teacher gathers data such as student test scores and evaluations of teaching by peers and supervisors, and makes adjustments in teaching style and practices.

The recommendation to keep a journal of teaching experiences can benefit veteran teachers as well as those new to the profession. By logging which teaching techniques were tried, students' reactions to them, and the teacher's appraisal of their effectiveness, a teacher has a personal record by which to judge the degree of success of instructional practices.

Change is necessary, not only for improving one's classroom teaching, but also for personal growth. Fred's readiness and ease in adopting state-of-the-art teaching equipment and materials could be attributed to the necessity of a positive attitude toward change in the world outside of teaching. His recognition that teaching tools such as the electronic whiteboard and Internet explorations are essential in reaching today's "digital" students underscores Fred's conviction that teachers must *reach* students in order to *teach* students.

Good teachers are open to change in order to meet the needs of students, whose world is changing rapidly. The change encountered by teachers refers not only to curriculum, materials, and teaching style, but also to the concept of "What is a school?" Fred offers his prediction about schools of the future, inviting the reader to speculate on the accelerated rate of change of schools in the twenty-first century compared to the barely perceptible change in the previous two centuries.

Fred's strong work ethic and commitment to his students are evident in his writing. Anyone who reads this book will find affirmation of the fact that being a teacher requires work far beyond the confines of the classroom or school day. Also evident is Fred's belief that student achievement, a respectful classroom environment, and job satisfaction make the hard work worthwhile.

The writing style of the book is conversational, rather than pedantic or my-way-is-the-only-way. I can imagine two teachers talking as I read the words. The teachers are sharing their wisdom, relating what works for them personally. That is what Fred Wootan does in *Not in My Classroom*. Enjoy your conversation with this teacher.

CHAPTER 1

Classroom Management— Not an Oxymoron

You walk around your classroom with a pen in hand and a pad in your shirt or blouse pocket. You talk to your class, stopping when necessary to listen while a student expresses his or her ideas. Meanwhile, other students turn toward you, anticipating your response, while others look at the questioning student, some with pens at the ready, and some already writing. Still others make muffled noises, carefully ruffling through papers, searching for something; something you know pertains to the discussion. Another student clicks away on one of the classroom computer's keyboards, while another looks over that student's shoulder whispering, suggesting a research site. All have textbooks opened on their desks along with small notebooks, and electronic voting pads.

The Smart Board on the front wall of the room shows examples of the material you are covering that day. Red, blue, and green marks on the board underline certain key words and mathematical symbols, clarifying your points. The whiteboard on another wall displays a schedule of events and assignments. Students' papers reflecting excellent grades are posted around the room.

The "hum" of active, participatory, and exciting learning in action permeates the space—a place you're proud to call "my classroom."

Sounds great in theory, doesn't it? Yet in practice, creating such a well-run, smooth-functioning learning environment requires classroom management skills far beyond those taught in education courses. In truth, many teachers find their classroom experience to be more like this:

The teacher lectures from behind a podium. He's dressed in professorial brown, complete with a narrow woolen tie. The monotonous sound of his voice fills the room. He looks as bored as he sounds. Some students stare blankly, slumping in their seats; others sleep outright. The smart ones look longingly out the window, wishing the rain would stop and they could leave. The troublemakers hang out in the back arguing over nothing and tormenting their fellow students. Nobody learns anything—except how to call for security when one of the troublemakers goes too far.

The Attempt to Establish Order

If you find yourself struggling to establish order so that you can actually *teach*, you are not alone. Every year in countless classrooms across America, teachers struggle to run their classrooms productively, effectively, and efficiently. More and more become frustrated by their inability to do so—and leave the profession.

Poor classroom management is at the root of the teaching profession's high burnout rate:

- The number of teachers leaving the profession exceeds the number of teachers who enter by 23 percent.
- Turnover is 32 percent higher than in non-teaching professions.
- Approximately one-third of America's teachers leave teaching sometime during their first three years.
- Almost one-half leave during the first five years.

The National Commission on Teaching and America's Future attributes these results to classroom management issues, such as poor administrative support, lack of teacher influence, classroom intrusions, and inadequate time.

It doesn't have to be this way. You *can* manage your classroom. You *can* motivate your students and change their lives for the better. You can give up baby-sitting your students, and start teaching them. All you need to do is master the principles of good classroom management, principles that can be applied in any classroom, no matter who your students, or where your school. You can do what you were meant to do—teach.

The Key Classroom Management Concepts

You thought that managing your classroom meant you simply kept order, got through your day's lesson, and had no interruptions from your demanding principal. You did this hoping that some of your students actually learned something they could use later on in their lives. This justified your exhaustion at the end of the day. Well, there's a lot more to it than that. In this book you'll not only learn how to achieve a great learning environment in your classroom, but will experience the personal satisfaction of a successful professional.

When you master the art of good classroom management, you'll create an atmosphere of mutual respect and an enthusiasm for learning that allows you to teach more than you ever dreamed possible. Your students will teach you in the process. You'll be a better teacher—and a better person.

In this book the key concepts of classroom management are laid out step by step. A great deal of the book focuses on planning and preparation, because a good teacher is a prepared teacher. You'll learn how to do the following:

Create Long-Term and Short-Term Plans

Good planning identifies your specific goals based on your knowledge of the school's goals, its facilities and services, the objective of your courses, and the potentials of your students as determined by a review of their portfolios.

Do Your Reconnaissance

Before the school year begins, you must visit your classroom to organize it—and to organize yourself. You want to
try to reduce or eliminate (okay, at least reduce) interruptions to your teaching process, beginning on the first day of
school. If you had this same classroom last year, take a hard
look at the organization of the room in light of your new
plan, and make the necessary changes in accordance with
that plan.

Wow Them on Opening Day

You must lay the groundwork with your students for the
year to come on that all-important first day. You want to make
the best possible first impression by the clothes you wear,
your welcoming speech, the rules you set down, and personal
remarks you exchange. Everything you do on this critical first
day communicates your seriousness, professionalism, enthusiasm, competence, and confidence—or lack thereof.

Establish Your Authority from the Get-Go

The basic precepts of good business management also
apply to you. You cannot lead people who don't want to be
led; you cannot manage people who don't recognize your
authority; and you cannot impart knowledge to people who
don't respect you. Your students want to know you, and want
you to know them as soon as possible. That presents a big
order if you have, say, one hundred or more new kids each
year. So how do you do it?

You will do it by enhancing your overall memorization
skills. You will use some proven name-learning methods such
as photographing students and studying available school
yearbooks, questionnaires, seating charts, and so on, so
that you can get to know your students and begin managing
your classroom as soon as possible. Just seeing you making
this effort to get to know them and make them aware of your
rules builds respect within your students. Even something as

simple as learning to pronounce and spell their names correctly is critical to gaining their respect.

Communicate the Rules

You'll learn how to lay down and enforce standards of behavior for major offenses such as classroom intrusions caused by a student carrying a weapon, bullying, seating arrangement disturbances, levels of boyfriends' and girlfriends' "friendliness," and rudeness.

Make Your Routine Their Routine

You'll learn how best to familiarize your students with your rules and your methods of controlling the paper flow, grading papers, communicating with parents, having individual conferences with students and parents, and establishing yourself as the leader of the classroom.

Create a Community of Learners

Establishing order in the classroom is only half the battle. Once you've got them in their seats, you must set their minds on fire. This book will show you all the techniques, strategies, and tools you need to make learning fun and profitable for every student—including you. You'll find innovative ways to motivate students to prevent boredom in the classroom, and to engage students with Attention Deficit Disorder (ADD), behavioral issues, and other problems.

Venture Outside the Classroom

Effective teachers maintain a sphere of influence far greater than their classrooms. There are myriad ways in which you can enrich the lives of your students outside the classroom. You can make your presence felt throughout the entire school and beyond by functioning as a club adviser. You also must venture out and continue *your* education, because a good teacher never stops learning. . . .

Build a Support Network

Your classroom is not an island—and you are not Tom Hanks. You must find ways to bond with other teachers, network with outside sources, learn effective speaking techniques, and gain an understanding of the national teaching environment to better understand your school and your role. You may also want to consider coaching one of the school sports teams, because sports fill a major role in overall student development.

Now It's Your Turn

Good classroom management depends on your awareness and knowledge of these concepts. Master these, and you'll run an exciting classroom in which students want to come and learn, and where you experience the happiness and fulfillment only gifted teachers enjoy. After all, it's that promise that drew you to teaching in the first place.

THE PROBLEM What do I do first to get started?

THE SOLUTION Take a good look around your world both inside and outside your classroom. Looking at the big picture will focus you on your part in it. Jot down your ideas as you read through this book.

Preparedness:
A Good Teacher Is a
Prepared Teacher

CHAPTER 2

Good Classroom Management Is in the Details:
Your Long-Range Plan for Success

You can't run a business without proper preparation. Okay, nobody said anything about running a business when you signed your teaching contract. And no one told you that teaching would be as stressful as juggling the management problems of sales, production, accounting, and meeting payroll either. But you had your suspicions, didn't you? You knew in your heart of hearts that a profession that offered three months' vacation every year must have stress connected with it somehow. Or, perhaps you've worked at this profession for many years now, and already know the stress is real. Reading this book will not completely dispel your suspicion or stress. It will, however, replace those negative feelings with a great feeling of satisfaction and accomplishment, as you learn to manage your classroom in much the same way that you would manage a business.

Classroom Management Compared to Management of a Business

Management, as defined in the world of business, means creating cooperative actions that function properly by converting disorganized people, machines, and money into a useful enterprise (you know, getting things done through other people). A business manager, like a teacher, must handle relationships outside and inside of the business. In business, those outside relationships consist of consumers, government, suppliers, and investors. Those inside are the executives, managers, and workers, each having its own dynamic. In the classroom the external relationships consist of the world at large, parents, benefactors (in private schools), and government. The internal relationships are the teachers, students, administrators, and other staff. Again, each has its own dynamic.

The successful manager must make changes in his or her business as necessary to react to changes in the marketplace in order for his or her goals to be realized. The process of management consists of planning, organizing, leading, and controlling. Good classroom management simply presents a variation of that theme. It applies those principles using the external demands of its customers: the parents and society.

THE PROBLEM I want to focus on my students and curriculum. All those outside influences can keep me from doing this.

THE SOLUTION Recognize that your classroom cannot fully function in isolation. The students are individuals with pressures from parents, coaches, part-time jobs, and more. All of these are your business. Embrace them; don't try to exclude or avoid them.

The Mission Statement of Your District

The world at large and, more specifically, the parents of your students are your customers and they demand you educate their child. The students represent the product of your effort. The school system of your state with all its parts provides the production facilities and must have a mission whether specifically stated or not. Generally speaking, that mission is to provide a source of education in compliance with the state's legal and educational regulations so that the students become productive citizens.

Your district must also have a mission statement, and it will read something like this: "It is the mission of this district to provide an education to develop productive citizens in compliance with the state legal and educational regulatory requirements, to increase the grades on the state standardized tests by 10 percent, and to reduce the dropout rate by 10 percent."

Each school must also have a mission statement that will, of necessity, be more specific. It will require, for example, that all teachers take continuing education in working with special needs children; that the school update the physical facilities to provide things such as air conditioning, to facilitate use in the summer months; conduct more frequent in-classroom teacher evaluations; and increase the graduation percentages and state standard testing scores to achieve top-level state standing. This mission will result in a one-year/five-year plan with specific, measurable goals. The statement of those goals will read like this: "The primary goal of the school is to raise student graduation percentages by 5 percent and lower the dropout rate to 4 percent by the end of the five years of the plan by mandating all teachers to take and to pass the local college courses 'Special Education in the Coming Decade,' 'Classroom Management,' and 'Teacher Motivation'; increase teacher classroom evaluations to five during the school year; and institute summer reading programs."

THE PROBLEM My school district's plan must have been written during the era of the one-room schoolhouse.

THE SOLUTION Look to the bigger picture either at the state or federal level to gain your focus.

Create Your Own Mission Statement

Read the school mission statement to determine how you will be evaluated, whether there are any continuing education requirements, and the number of expected classroom evaluations. At minimum, you want to be able to comply with its requirements. But what do you do if your school has no apparent mission?

You establish your own goals, but instead of basing your mission statement on that of the school, you base it on the educational mission of our nation. The summation of our nation's educational goals can best be stated with the following quotation, attributed to Lord Brougham: "Education makes a people easy to lead, but difficult to drive; easy to govern, but impossible to enslave." Only with an informed populace can a nation survive and thrive over the long run. Therefore, it falls upon you, the teacher, to provide the information to expand the young minds of our nation. You must know your subject and exercise good judgment so your students will allow that knowledge into their minds.

Now you're ready to develop a mission statement that includes continuing professional development and good classroom management techniques. Do this and you will happily work at this wonderful profession for many years. Your mission statement will look like this: "My mission is to educate students in the most professional manner possible by availing myself of every opportunity to improve my teaching methods, and applying these in my classroom so my students will have the greatest opportunity for a lifetime of learning."

THE PROBLEM I thought my mission was to teach arithmetic, a subject that hasn't changed since its beginning.

THE SOLUTION Arithmetic may not have changed, but students and our society certainly have. Keep yourself abreast of current world and local events in order to gain perspective. Attend seminars on new teaching methods for instructing a populace raised on video games and with computers.

Create Your Plan Based on Your Mission Statement

Start the school year well before the school opens by preparing for it properly. Doing this takes only a few hours away from your summer relief, and gives you the confidence to begin the year smiling, ready with the classroom management skills you need to achieve the satisfaction of a job well done. Your preparation will make you feel like a successful new teacher who worked so hard in college, or like a revitalized, experienced teacher. More important, your students will experience a new level of learning. If you do not plan, then you plan to fail. Instead, succeed by planning from the start.

Based upon your mission statement, you begin to develop your plan. A good plan must be achievable, measurable, and involve research of the field of study. The businessman would say that you must plan, organize, lead, and control. The real measure of your success may not come until a student succeeds at a given goal or profession because of the foundation of knowledge you provided. It's possible that you may never know whether your students achieved success after their school years. So how will you measure the success of your plan? You will measure it by establishing your goals for subject matter and by testing the students for comprehension of your material, recording benchmarks along the way.

THE PROBLEM My mission statement takes care of any planning I need other than my daily lesson plans.

THE SOLUTION The mission statement is like the name of your business. It identifies it.

The businessman must know where the economy is going in order to know how or when to change his or her production facilities in order to be successful. You must know what it takes to educate kids this year, and what changes you need to make to educate them next year and beyond. That's called planning.

You're the Expert Now, but Take These Steps Anyway

You must know your subject, look like you know your subject, and teach it. You will be amazed how much you will learn during your early years in this profession. (I found it hard to believe that I didn't already know it all when I first started. But then, that's me, not you.)

First, it should go without saying that you must have the basic knowledge in a subject from your college course of study. In addition to that, you should read past texts and old lesson plans, and reflect on the changes. If you've taught for many years, take a serious look back to the materials previously used for teaching your courses, and compare those to what you teach with today.

Also look at the course itself and recognize its changes. Most of the time changes take place over such a long period of time that they go unnoticed. If you find you can't remember the reason for making your changes, study your old lesson plans. Why? Because how you teach during the coming year will be affected by those changes. If you can't see much difference in the course texts and other materials, then you should contact the author(s) or publisher to learn the reasoning. Why? Because those changes very likely involved societal pressures rather than actual changes in the subject matter.

For example, you may have a new English book this year. It focuses on writings aligned with important historical periods such as the American Revolution, the American Civil War era, World War II, and space travel, just to name a few. The writers you study should be those who formed the basis of literary thought as a result of those historical changes. For example, our country had a serious antiwar backlash over its involvement in the Vietnam War.

Such writers as Lawrence Ferlinghetti wrote poetry and prose after World War II, Sputnik, and the Vietnam War. Ferlinghetti became the central figure in the "Beat" movement of the 1950s and 1960s. He sent out the message that the citizens of this country should free themselves from conventional traditions such as marriage. Ambrose Bierce, better known as "Bitter Bierce," felt that too many of the important writings after the Civil War romanticized heroism and courage, thereby justifying the atrocities of that war. One of his writings, "An Occurrence at Owl Creek Bridge," used psychological fiction and flashback to show the darker side of that war. Certainly, everyone knew the darker side. What they needed was to see it in contrast to the romantic visions portrayed by many other writers.

From this example, you see the importance of knowing history even when teaching English. It also should help you understand how important your depth of knowledge in many subjects becomes.

What If I'm Not an Expert?

If you're *not* an expert—say you majored in English and the principal signs you up to teach a math course (which would happen only in an extreme emergency in most school systems), you need to brush up on your college algebra. Get the math text you will use. Study the chapter and section questions for familiarization. Work the problems to make sure you know the formulas.

Don't slight this area. If you don't know your subject, the kids will catch on, and guess where their level of respect and attention will go.

Tips for Getting Ready

Once you have studied your background material and your course curriculum, you can begin with the steps that follow. Obviously, these may vary depending on the age level you will teach.

1. Read background material. Review any outside material you feel will build your background, and also decide on the outside reading you want for the students.

2. Review government standards. Review the standards of both your school and the state so you will at least achieve those as an absolute minimum.

3. Count pages. Check the number of pages in the text you will use. Divide that number by four for quarters, or thirds for trimesters, to determine the number of pages per quarter or trimester. This may sound like an oversimplification, but if you are a first-year teacher who doesn't know how long it takes to lecture on a topic, counting pages provides a place to start. For you veterans it will provide a foundation and a measurement for what you have tried to do in the past.

4. Read text material sorted by grading period. Read the material for each quarter and make adjustments to pages based on the level of difficulty you anticipate. Factor in the time for required outside reading, videos, audio-visual demonstrations, field trips, and any other resources you think will enhance the learning.

5. Obtain the school calendar of events for the school year. This will show you when the primary interruptions to your classes occur. Your school will have field trips, club and service activities for the students, cultural events in the auditorium, in-service days, days off for holidays, and on and on. Generally the principal will make no exceptions to these.

6. Purchase a recording device. I bought a digital recorder that fits in my shirt pocket, has oodles of memory and files, and replays clearly, all for under $75. (Maybe your school will provide this.) An interesting hidden benefit of using this device can surface if you record while holding class, as I have done. I had actually recorded several classes in order to find out whether I had any irritating speaking mannerisms such as saying "okay" frequently, or "umm" while thinking about an answer. The hidden benefit came to light a few days later, when I reminded the students of something I had said during that previous class. One student said he knew I hadn't told them that because he didn't have it in his notes. I told him that I had said it six times, to be exact (I had just by chance listened to the recording before that class), and asked if he would like for me to play the recording. That answer may sound curt, and it was (I knew this student well, and curt answers were the only kind he understood). So was the student's comment. By that time most of the class was scrambling, looking at their notes, and saying to him that they had the information I had asked for. He started writing it down immediately. The importance of that incident wasn't that I had a recording to prove my statements, but that most of that class had gotten my statement and written it in their notebooks when I said it the first time. That is what I call a moment of success; minor success, but success nonetheless. They actually took notes. I know that not everyone in my classes writes everything I say in their notebooks, at least I hope not, but they were at least writing the important things.

7. Practice and record your lectures. If you teach math or science, practice solving sample problems or conducting experiments while you talk. The recorder will indicate the time involved. Add 25 to 30 percent of this time for questions and interruptions. Listen to the recording for the volume, inflections in your voice, and idiosyncrasies in your patterns of speech. Did you repeatedly say "okay," "umm," or anything that sounded irritating? Did you sound interested in your subject? If not, the students won't find it interesting either.

8. Practice lectures in your classroom, preferably several days before school starts. Record your practice lectures, and then place the recorder in the front of the room. Start playing back the lecture, and walk to the back of the room, to the most distant seat from where you lecture. Can you hear it? (There's more about preparing in your classroom in Chapter 3.) Did that "enthusiasm for the course" come through? If not, you know what to do.

9. Write that long-range plan. Everything you need is now in place. List the things you want to accomplish during the year. For example, you want to have the students gain experience in writing literary analysis and the five different kinds of essays; or to have the students experience learning and experimenting with the basic elements of science; or you want them to be able to converse with each other, at least in simple sentences, using French; or you want them to become good public speakers who are also capable debaters. Remember, your plan must be specific, attainable, and measurable.

You're the Judge and Jury Now—Exercise Good Judgment in Grading

Make sure your students know how you read their work, and consistently apply the same logic of evaluation throughout the year, and you will have good, nonprejudicial classroom judgment. One way to help make sure the grades have no prejudice is to block out the student's name while grading. Require that they all place their name, class block, and date in the same place on their papers. Use the upper right corner even if you think this sounds trivial. Take care of the little things, and the big things won't cause such stress and trauma and student concern for the fairness of your grading. Unfortunately, grades drive the study. A recent survey of several students asked about "learning" and grades, and most of them equated the two. Rarely will you find a student in elementary or high school who really wants to learn just to gain knowledge and is ambivalent toward grades. So, for most students, the importance of using this method of grading cannot be overemphasized. Parents will say that their primary interest for their child is learning, but having said that, grades really "float their boat." They'll say you can't get into a good college with poor grades. At least until someone comes up with something better, grades are the guideline. Grades also provide the sign of success in learning and in your good judgment. (Evaluation of student work not only provides grades for the students, but can also give a teacher insight into how well he is teaching the material.)

You must discipline fairly, and you must not distinguish among students when it comes to classroom behavior. One of the first things your new students ask isn't "How do you discipline," but "How do you grade?" They then quickly follow with, "How hard is this course?" Let's take the second question first.

Smile and tell them nicely they should ask someone who has just taken the class. Then tell them you have confidence that, if they pay attention, and do the assignments, they will learn the material.

The first question generally does not address the school's grading scales unless you have first-time students in the school. This question actually asks whether you give tests, or homework, or classroom assignments, and what value you place on each, or whether you just lecture and expect them to get it. It also implies what the students already know happens, which is that exceptions always come into the picture. So, how do you handle these? Are you going to be fair?

THE PROBLEM New students always ask, "How do you grade?"

THE SOLUTION Tell them you grade fairly and to ask a student who has just taken your class.

Develop a Grading Strategy That Works, Part I

Remind your students of the school's grading policies, such as giving letter grades based on numerical calculations of the students' work. For example, an A represents a numerical score from 90 percent to 100 percent; a B is 80 percent to 89 percent; and so on. Obviously you need a method of your own which will, in turn, allow you to explain your system. Questions to ponder for your grading strategy:

1. **Scale to use:** Are you going to grade everything on a percentage scale, such as a grade of 100 percent for excellent work, and on down to a zero for no work?

2. **Homework:** What value do you want to place on homework? Will you check it to determine the student's accuracy, or just to acknowledge that they completed it?

3. **Writing assignments:** Do you place a value on writing assignments for language arts equal to or less than objective tests on the text material?

4. **Keeping up in math or science:** If you teach math or science, how are you going to handle the student who can't quite keep up but tries really hard?

5. **Students need to know current events:** Do the students really need to know current events in social studies?

6. **Is writing really necessary?** Must all the students learn to write legibly at the same time?

7. **What about late assignments?** Will you accept them, reduce the grade for lateness, or not accept them after a certain number of days late?

8. **How about missed tests?** When does the student have to make them up? Does making up tests also apply to pop quizzes? How about a student with high absenteeism?

You get the idea. Consider these questions before the start of the school year, because the kids all expect equal and fair treatment, especially in this area. Don't panic, but don't neglect developing this part of your plan, which makes you the one who determines standards of equality and fairness. If you don't do this, the kids will. And rest assured, they will each have a different viewpoint of fairness.

THE PROBLEM My students are always saying that my grading is not fair. I tell them that it is fair and they just have to trust me, but I feel uncomfortable with that answer.

THE SOLUTION Your plan of developing a consistent grading formula and taking a few minutes to explain it to them periodically will eliminate those questions.

Create a Grading Strategy That Works, Part II

Answering the questions in the preceding lists develops one part of your grading strategy. The other part depends on your evaluation of the skills you teach. In each discipline, the specific values may vary. In English, for example, development of good writing skills commands the highest value. Someday the students may need to communicate by writing a very important message, so they must learn the basics of clarity, grammar, syntax, spelling, and good overall writing techniques. They will learn these skills as the teacher helps them understand what the great writers have written, all the while asking themselves why the author used those particular words, phrases, allusions, alliterations, and so on.

Create Focus Using Percentages as Values

That focus determines the basic valuation system for grading. For an English class, it would be as follows:

- Writing assignments—value 30 percent.
- Tests on text techniques of writing—value 30 percent.
- Vocabulary quizzes based on a vocabulary study book—value 10 percent.
- Read and grade homework based on correctness of the answers to the questions asked in the text, thereby verifying whether or not the student understood what he or she read—value 10 percent.
- Classroom participation (more about this later)—value 20 percent.

There you have it. The percentage-basis grading technique develops total values of 100 percent.

Create Focus Using Numerical Calculations

Some teachers prefer using the mathematical point system. As an example, assuming the same value system as the one above, they would allow for a student to accumulate something like 1,000 points each quarter. That would mean they would allocate 300 points to writing assignments, 300 points to text tests, 100 points to vocabulary quizzes, 100 points to homework, and 200 points to classroom participation. The kids like this system because it allows them to keep track of their points and, therefore, have a good idea of what their final grade will be. This system would be difficult for a beginning teacher because of lack of past experience in selecting the maximum number. Here's where building a support system of veteran teachers—which will be discussed later—comes in handy.

Nothing is ever as simple as it appears. Let's look at some of the variations that can come up in grading strategies and focuses so you can plan for them. The following list does not include every possibility, but covers many of the potential problems:

- No matter what course or courses you teach, some kids will be absent on the day of a test. If your policy allows them to make up the test as long as they do so within about ten days (but certainly before the end of the grading period), do not return the tests to the rest of the class until the absent students have made it up. You may find that, with your group of kids, you must require they make up a test within one week, or they will let it go until the end of the grading period, leaving you with an influx of tests to grade quickly.

    You can guess what will happen if you simply allow them to miss a test. Suddenly, on every test day you will have a nearly empty classroom. Give students a zero (0) if they don't make up the test within your time frame. (A grade of zero on a test can put a student hopelessly in the hole grade-wise, so you may want to consider giving a minimum grade such as 50 percent or 60 percent instead of the zero.)

- For lengthy writing assignments such as a literary analysis, distribute the assignment requirements well in advance (six weeks will work) and require your students to turn in the final paper on a specific date. (Since all kids procrastinate, have them show you their outline after four weeks, and their rough draft after five weeks.) Every day after that day (including weekends and holidays) deduct some percentage (say, 10 percent).

- When assigning students presentations for class, you must require the students to be there on the day of the presentation and to give their presentations on that day. In the case of a group assignment, give each member in the group a specific part of the assignment. If any group member misses class on the required presentation day, the others must give it without that student. The absent student then has the obligation to make his or her own individual presentation at the next class when he or she returns or receive a zero (0).

- A student comes to you on the due date of a major writing assignment and tells you his or her computer crashed, or the printer ran out of ink, or some other calamity occurred. What you do depends on the explanation as to why he or she just discovered the problem the day before the paper's due date (make sure you ask this). This means you need to get to know your students early on, and well (more about this in Chapter 8) Because some students will abuse the ability to make excuses, many teachers make no exceptions to the due date.

- A student with a track record of timeliness comes to you the day before a big paper's due date and tells you a grandparent died, obviously causing a sad distraction for the entire family. What do you do? Choosing to believe that student builds the bond between you and that student, making it worthwhile to give him or her a break. Again, you need to know the student.

- A student comes to you on the due date of a big paper telling you he or she cannot finish it on time and gives you a reason, which may or may not be true. You have the option to tell him or her to turn in the paper the next day or later, and that may work fine. Be careful. Remember fairness.

- How about the good student who, on the last week of school, contracts some kind of virus or flu illness and misses that critical week filled with year-end work and the final exam? You call the parents to confirm, and make an appropriate exception. You will need to inform the office that the student will receive an incomplete grade that you will finalize at a later date. Make sure you know the school policy on these matters.

- What do you do with the student who has a belligerent attitude, and who constantly causes trouble, even telling you never to send him or her to the office or home? That's a tough one, but you need to prepare for this by knowing the school policy. There will be more on that later.

THE PROBLEM Sometimes I must make an exception to my grading rules, and doing that has a potential for what students may perceive as unfairness.

THE SOLUTION Don't forget who makes the rules. The student's perception of fairness is always self-centered. If you make exceptions rarely and after careful consideration, the occasional exception will not become a problem.

Learn Your School Rules

Although there are as many examples as there are students, by now you get the message of preparedness based on your initial definition of fairness. Let's move on to examples of rules that your school may have, and how to meld yours into them. Every school will have written rules of behavior, grading scales, attendance requirements, behavior in the halls, scholastic requirements to participate in sports (influenced by NCAA and state athletic association requirements), your attendance and availability to students and parents for conferences, and so on. These rules will provide the basis for some of your classroom rules. Here are some examples of school rules:

- **No cheating.** Again, you need to apply a diligent effort, especially regarding cheating on tests, and whether the consequences for cheating on tests will apply to homework, writing assignments, and group projects as well.
- **No chewing gum in the building.** Okay, that clearly means you may not permit gum-chewing in your classroom.
- **No smoking on the school campus.** Now you must not only monitor your classroom, but anywhere you may go on campus. Must you go searching for violators? No, but naiveté won't endear you to the principal or other faculty.
- **Students must have a pass signed by the teacher to go into the hallway during class periods.** Make sure you have a supply of the forms the school requires if you intend to permit a student to go to the bathroom, the office, or other places during class.

Develop Your Own Specific Classroom Rules (Yes, You May!)

When you create your own classroom rules, be sure that they coincide with those of the school. (Chapter 7 covers this area in depth.) Don't create conflict, because that always increases the stress level for you, and for your principal, and for the students. By all means, develop rules that are specific to your classroom and your personality. But don't, for example, allow gum-chewing in your classroom. Don't overlook cheating or acts of plagiarism; they not only violate the school rules, but also have legal repercussions.

Remember that whether you teach at a public or private school, it must have rules that are supported by the laws in this country. Your principal probably won't be enamored with you if you consistently allow your students to violate the school rules.

THE PROBLEM The school has a "no gum" policy, but I don't mind if my students chew gum during class.

THE SOLUTION Follow the school rules. Do not let your classroom become the exception. If the school does not allow gum-chewing, you should not allow gum-chewing.

Okay, let's sum up what we know so far:

1. Mission determines your raison d'être, your reason to exist, so let's not overlook it before trying to establish any sort of plan.
2. You must develop an achievable and measurable plan for the school year and for five years going forward. Once you have your one-year/five-year plan in place, you can develop your short-range plan down to the daily lessons.
3. In order to properly plan you must know your subject and know your ability to deliver based on the time allotted. You cannot teach what you don't know, so when you find that your principal has assigned you to teach a course for which you were not trained, you must get the training.
4. Prepare to make exceptions to your grading plan based on your judgment of fairness and consistency of application of that judgment.
5. You must know the school rules in order to properly establish and enforce your classroom rules.

Now you're ready to establish your short-range plan for each grading period, and within that, the specific lessons for each class period.

CHAPTER 3

Good Classroom Management Is in the Sum of the Details:
Your Short-Range Plan for Success

You may now begin looking at the parts that made up your long-range plan. If, for example, your long-range plan called for a 2 percent increase in the state standard test scores the first year and 5 percent over a total of five years, that's a good focal point because it's certainly a measurable goal. Now you need to break down that annual goal chronologically, starting with quarters. If you've taught for a number of years without this type of planning, you will find this specific goal orientation a great way to develop excellent lesson plans, and to better evaluate your results. If you're just beginning your teaching career, you will find it a great way to start. A famous person once wrote that you begin a voyage by taking the first step; an even more famous (or perhaps infamous) person wrote that teaching, like running a business, requires a lot of preparation.

Typically, school academic plans are based on two major grading periods, called semesters. We won't start there because that's too big a chunk of time, and also because semesters are also typically divided in halves, or quarters— periods of nine weeks. Let's start with the quarter, and follow with weekly, and then daily plans.

The Quarterly Plan

You have already clearly stated your mission and annual plans based on the required curriculum. You must now work on a shorter time period to accomplish your goals.

Work with One Course at a Time

For the sake of clarity and ease of following through on this in a precise and logical manner, use one period at a time with each course. The first period is the quarter, followed by the week, then the day, with English being the course.

Take the assigned text for this course and go to the table of contents. (Assume that the content of the textbook is closely aligned to the course of study for the class and covers the objectives in your plan for the year.) Scanning it, you may find it contains a thousand pages with five parts or sections and twenty chapters (I'll keep the math simple in this example). Scan the main divisions and you will likely find that parts four and five both have fewer pages than do each of the preceding three parts. That was no accident. The authors knew that the kids would wear down throughout the year, and shortened the lessons as their school year concluded.

Because of this you can squeeze those two shorter parts into the last quarter. So you have a textbook from which you segregated one part per quarter for the first three quarters, and two parts followed by the final exam for the last quarter.

You must provide a consistent approach if at all possible, and using the parts and chapters accomplishes this. Obviously, everyone needs to look deeper. You math, science, art, history, music, and technology teachers may think this simplistic approach won't work for your courses. Hang on. Your courses build throughout the year, becoming more complex, potentially meaning that you could cover more pages at the beginning of the year than at the end. Make any adjustments you need to accommodate the content.

Many books aren't set up as neatly as the one in our example. Think of this process as you would a sudoku puzzle. Logic using numbers allows for an orderly and even spread of instruction. It breaks down a textbook into easily manageable and understandable chunks. It also permits you to visualize each task. If you can see it, you can explain it better. Now scan the chapters to look for the most logical flow of information. Dividing up the book by pages, parts, and chapters is definitely an oversimplification, but that's okay for now. It's the first step in this business of teaching, making it easier to see how everything fits together. And, if you can see it, there is a good possibility your students will also see it, especially if you carefully point them to it.

You will learn more about this subject later in this book. At this point it suffices to say that the most important thing you can do is to set up your course of study in such a way that you can sell it to your students. Yes, you must sell the students on your knowledge of the course, and why they need to take your course. They won't get it if you don't tell them.

THE PROBLEM There was no assigned textbook for this class.

THE SOLUTION Research the topic and bring together all the reference material you can find.

You Are a Salesperson

Okay, you thought you were a teacher—and you are. Look at it this way. Can you remember when you went to elementary or high school? There you were sitting in class, wondering why you had to take this stupid course. If you haven't experienced that, have you ever overheard your students asking this same question? Or, maybe some of you have actually had a student raise his or her hand and boldly ask that question in front of the whole class. Don't forget, it's the student you want to educate, and you can't educate someone who doesn't want it. In the business management world I heard over and over at various seminars that you can't lead anyone who doesn't want to follow. You can't manage people who don't want you to manage them, and you can't sell a product to someone who sees no need for it.

At this point it is very important that you understand that your students need the information you provide. There must be a logical flow of the information you provide, so that you can succeed with that all-important selling job. Your students must feel it so they will buy into it. Some of you will find yourselves in front of a diversified audience, some will not, but it doesn't matter whether your audience consists of kids from upper-class, middle-class, or lower-class backgrounds. You must convince them they want what you have to sell, or you might as well find other employment.

You Really Have Something They Want; Tell Them

Once we have become acquainted, I tell students that I spent more than thirty-five years working in corporate America, holding every position from entry level to president of a company, and also owning my own company. Those incredulous looks on their faces tell me they cannot understand why I am there, and, more important, why I am telling them my story. The point of my story comes out when I tell them that in all those years I noticed a continued deterioration in the written use of our beautiful language, especially among the younger people. But I add that I also saw it in the higher levels of corporations among supposedly highly educated people. That is truly sad. So, I left that world to do what I could to turn that around, even if only in a small way, in one high school. Now there is no place in the world I would rather be than in that classroom with them, and they will get the best from me that I have to offer. If they will work with me, I will teach them good writing techniques, expand their vocabularies, and add to their appreciation of great literature, and they will gain a tremendous respect from the adult world because of it.

You may have a different story to tell, but you can get the same message across. Everyone wants respect for who they are. Your message is that you respect your students enough to teach them to the best of your ability.

THE PROBLEM The kids can be squirrelly. Sometimes I just can't seem to get them to settle down and listen to me.

THE SOLUTION Your silence will get their attention, especially if you stand in their midst. Once they have stopped fidgeting and talking, and they will, don't lecture them on their bad attitude. Thank them for settling down, and move on with your class.

Begin all this process before the first day of school by making your "honey do" list.

Make Your Own "Honey Do" List

Those of you who are married probably already know what a "honey do" list is, so you can take a couple of minutes' breather. Those who haven't experienced the joy of a "honey do" list should pay attention here. Quite simply, a "honey do" list is a list of household chores that need to be done. This list finds its way onto a conspicuous thing in the home so the husband is sure to see it—you guessed it, on the refrigerator door. *Okay, everyone, come on back.*

Start your year with your "honey do" list of the benefits of taking your course, so you don't forget anything. Post the list in a prominent place for all to see. When the school year has passed and the students reread the list, they will be amazed that they once asked, "Why do I have to take this course?"

I have even had kids come to me at the end of the year and say they can't believe that they read the whole book and still managed to accomplish several writing assignments and analyze four novels. The feeling of accomplishment that shows on their faces lights my fire for wanting to get through the summer and start anew with another group.

Write the Best Short-Range Plan of Your Career

The quarterly plan—derived from the annual—presents a much more manageable amount of material to cover. Having the mission and long-term plan to run on makes it so much easier to become precise in what you want to accomplish. Be warned that, even before you finish the first-quarter plan, you will begin thinking about the second-quarter plan. Then you'll begin thinking about the next quarter and semester and how you may need to adjust your long-range plan. Write good notes as your thoughts wander into the future, all the while keeping your primary focus on the quarter at hand.

Start your process in June after you spend a couple of weeks recharging your batteries. During that time, your subconscious will work on its own. Begin taking notes by blue-skying, and then researching details of the long-range plan. Put those notes aside until a couple of weeks before school starts. When that time comes along, you will be at the peak of readiness.

THE PROBLEM Summer is always over before I am ready, and I can't seem to get my plans together.

THE SOLUTION Write down your notes about the past year a couple of weeks after it has ended. This may take a few hours. Then enjoy the summer. When school starts, those notes will trigger your plans. Your subconscious will have worked all summer and will be ready.

Look Back to Move Forward

If you're a beginning teacher, look back at your college course work and student teaching. Think about the significance of the courses, the way your teaching mentor taught, and put yourself in that picture. If you are an experienced teacher, look back at the previous year or years. Compare the results of several years if possible. Think about how class dynamics affected the results of your teaching. Look back before looking forward, and adjust your plan to fit the time and dimension of the class.

Then take a look at your annual plan and see if you have considered new, measurable goals. You may discover that your results were less than satisfactory but were unsure why. Kind of like that "honey do" list of chores at home. Weigh the value of those less than successful against the good ones.

Scan last year's planner for "hiccups," times when you blew it or really got off track. Yes, that will happen. More than likely those hiccups resulted from the influence of outside factors: you suffered a family crisis or illness; your school had facility problems, like a heating system that failed in mid-winter, closing the school for several days; the kids in the grade you teach did something spectacular for the community and received a trip that lasted a couple of days; one of your classes had difficulty keeping up with your schedule, and you had to slow their pace. Hiccups don't normally repeat themselves every year. You must take that into account when looking forward.

Now calculate your school days from your school calendar. Deduct holidays, in-service days, and recurring events for the students that take them away from your classroom. This nets down to the quarterly class periods and thus, the class hours available to you. Now, to get your arms around the amount of material you can cover, set up an outline. No matter the course you teach, start with a heading that reads "first quarter." Drop down half a page and enter "week one." Skip a quarter of a page and enter "week two," and keep skipping quarter pages and entering until you have entered the nine weeks of the quarter.

Return to the text you will use and begin skimming the first part and the first three chapters that you want to cover during this quarter. Keeping your annual priorities in mind, find the chapters that best fit those priorities and enter them on the page immediately after the "first quarter" entry, leaving a few lines between each. Look over the table of contents, scanning the details of information covered by that first part.

For example, in my junior English class the text starts with the basic elements of writing, and that just happens to fit perfectly with my philosophy of getting the basics down first, and then building on them. So I write "basic techniques—poetry, fiction, nonfiction, drama" as my first entry, leaving a line or two between each.

Continuing to scan topics, I recognize that the book covers American literature chronologically, and so my next entries consist of topics from the first four chapters, beginning with "Origins of the American Traditions," circa 1700, and ending with "The New England Renaissance," around 1860. Included in those topics are poems and short stories to read and analyze.

As with most courses, not everything comes directly from the textbook. I know I want the students to analyze and write a paper on a novel as well as two essays, and study vocabulary words from another text. So I enter the name of the book, the essay types, and, after reviewing the vocabulary book the same as the textbook, I enter "Chapters 1–4 vocabulary." I think about how long it will take for the students to critically read the novel so that they can properly analyze it. I decide on a date when I want to receive the written report and enter that. I want to spread out writing assignments evenly throughout the quarter, so I enter the types and dates for them.

Now I must consider how many readings the class can properly handle. I review all that are available in the text, pick them in the order of importance, and enter their titles. I also add titles of readings from outside sources I want to cover. Finally, I want to teach some speaking skills, so I know I want to have each student give a short speech. The speech will of necessity have to occur near the end of the quarter because I will need to get to know my students well enough to pick speech topics that they will find relevant and interesting. I enter a date for speeches. You can use these examples as a guideline for putting your items into a weekly order.

THE PROBLEM I lay out everything as logically and chronologically as possible. Experience tells me it won't work out that way, and I can never seem to get back to my original target.

THE SOLUTION Did I forget to tell you that you are shooting at a moving target? You must be flexible. Take regular looks at where you are in order to determine priorities for going forward.

Your Weekly Plan

You know how many total class hours you have for the quarter, so divide that number by nine to arrive at your weekly class hours. Do the same for the readings you have entered and spread them into each week. Enter the writing dates into the corresponding week.

Enter subject titles into your outline template. Take a look at how much instruction will be necessary for the book analysis and essays. Enter those lecture topics chronologically into the proper weeks. The last item is vocabulary, and you spread the four vocabulary quizzes in the proper weeks. You are now ready to set up your daily planner.

Your Daily Plan

Wouldn't it be great if you knew exactly what to enter into your daily planner? You know that if you have a daily planner, your stress level drops dramatically. Guess what? Since you have an outline of what you want to teach already written out on a weekly basis, this part of the job should be like shooting fish in a bowl. Here's the best way to do it.

Plan It Like a Speech

Have you ever given a speech? Okay, I'll assume you haven't. If you were giving a speech, you would take memory joggers to the podium with you. You would want them easily accessible, and you would *really* want the ability to read them with little or no difficulty so the audience would hardly notice. How does this apply to your daily planning? Just stick with the outline you already have set up on the weekly basis. Estimate your lecture times, group project times, testing times, and other minor activities. Let's continue with my English class example.

The daily lesson plan done in summary outline form is best. You don't really want to plan out your exact lecture or group activities down to who will partner up and how long each student has to spend on doing his or her part in the project. Just plan the amount of time you intend to lecture on the subject and/or allow for your students to discuss their project. If you do want them to work in groups, groups of three work best. One leads, one transcribes, and one researches. If you put a fourth in groups they tend to play.

Read the selections from the text that you want to read and discuss in class. Time yourself when reading and answering the discussion questions. Figure that it will take about twice as long as that to do it in class, allowing for distractions and extraneous questions. We have eighty-minute blocks for our classes. A typical lesson plan for one class could look like this in my calendar: Start time 8:40—1 min—meditation; 2 min— attend.; 5 min—review HW ques. "Pit & Pendulum," Poe, add 20 min. discuss.; 10 min—lec. Gothic genre & period; 15 min—lit. tech; 5 min—vocabs/wk; 12 min— P.O.V. & writing skills & how to write Gothic essay; 10 min to summarize their notes & show to me; next for HW read "An Occurrence at Owl Creek Bridge" by Bierce; write answers to the questions at the end of the piece.

Here it is written out: One minute to say or read a meditation to calm everyone; two minutes to take attendance; five minutes to collect and record homework, which consisted of written answers to discussion questions at the end of the story "The Pit and the Pendulum" by Edgar Allan Poe; then allow twenty minutes to discuss those questions and some of my own; follow with a ten-minute lecture on the Gothic genre and the time period when Poe wrote this piece; follow with a fifteen-minute discussion of the literary techniques used by Gothic writers to prepare the students for writing a Gothic essay; five minutes for reviewing vocabulary words from the vocabulary book and asking students to write the words in a sentence to get at the connotative definitions; twelve minutes lecturing on point-of-view and essay writing skills in the Gothic genre (notice the writing skills repeats from earlier); ten minutes for students to summarize their notes and show them to me; write on the whiteboard the homework assignment to read "An Occurrence at Owl Creek Bridge" by Ambrose Bierce and do the discussion questions. You see why you can't really write everything out, but you must have it all there. I like to have every minute planned because their time is precious, and I don't want to waste even one minute.

The Best Planning Tool: The Computerized Calendar

I know you love your daily planner, but still, you should take a look at the available electronic calendars. I use Microsoft Works Suite, which includes a calendar; a Works word processor for writing papers and letters; a spreadsheet; a Works database, which has an address book, a form for keeping inventory (school books); MSN for accessing the Internet, and much more. Similar software packages include Microsoft Office; WebEx WebOffice for PCs; Mac OS X iCal for Macintosh; Make Your Own Calendar by Creative Computer Solutions for Window and Macintosh.

Keep it simple. What you need to be able to do is schedule everything you could possibly cover in as short a time frame as possible, and then adjust as the quarter progresses. You also want easy, portable access and minimal information, such as date, time, name of class, curriculum to cover during that specific time, and homework and writing assignments. All of these software programs fulfill those needs and will save you time to allow an occasional round of golf, thereby maintaining some semblance of a life outside the classroom.

Using the electronic calendar not only benefits you, but aids in keeping parents and guardians informed of assignments. If your school has a Web site, you should be able to post your calendar to it.

You may also post details of all assignments to the site, announce marching band practices, and on and on, so that when the students lose the written instructions or announcements, they can look them up on the school site. If you do post information to the site, notify all parents of its availability, and don't forget to keep it current.

Additionally, doing this creates an opportunity to either learn more about the Web or, if you don't have the time or inclination, to get a student to help, providing him or her with valuable experience and also building a greater bond with that student.

You may also want to consider using the Web site to support collaboration on the curriculum. If, for example, you teach history and are currently studying the era of the Civil War, and at the same time the English department is studying the literature of that period, the art department the artistic works, and the music department the development of music as influenced by that war, your school could have an area on its Web site for display of curriculum collaboration. Assignments connected with that period would be posted in there. The students would have to go to that site to get their assignments, and would automatically make the connection among those courses.

Of course, simply posting these assignments on one place on the Web site will not make those connections for the students. You still must teach the connections; the Web site simply reinforces your teaching, allowing students to learn, for example, why it's important to know that Frederick Douglass wrote about his life as a slave, and why his style of writing made a difference in what he had to say. Again, the computerized calendar can be the pathway to assembling this information. Give serious thought to how you could use an electronic calendar to increase your efficiency as well as create a broader learning experience for the students. Everything you can do in the way of daily planning will enhance the overall learning environment, and reduce "hiccups" and classroom downtime.

THE PROBLEM By the end of the school year my daily planner looks like chickens walked all over it from all the changes. I really have difficulty using it for planning.

THE SOLUTION An electronic calendar allows changes to be made easily and neatly.

What May Go Wrong

Even when you've planned everything out, things won't go perfectly!

The Best-Laid Plans . . . Go Amuck

Often even the best plans go amuck, for as many reasons as you have students in your classroom. Let's take a look at the example of my English class, because some students become confused on the work for that period, and particularly on writing in the Gothic genre. For example, when writing a Gothic essay you need suspense. Creating suspense is very difficult for young, inexperienced writers. Their tendency is to tell what is going to happen too soon, thereby unintentionally relieving the tension and killing the suspense. I spend twenty or so minutes lecturing and explaining how to maintain the suspense. When it gets close to the end of the period, I allow the students time to summarize their notes.

You Gotta Be Flexible

Flexibility is an absolute necessity, so when you have the annual plan out there in front of you, that's the time to mark the most important items to cover. You already did this if you read the earlier part of this chapter, but now reinforce it by taking a second look before class starts. You must decide on the goal of each class, depending on the level of students enrolled. Is this a college-prep class? Or are these students preparing to enter the workforce directly after high school? This really does matter because you need to decide whether you are getting them ready for higher learning, or laying a basic fundamental foundation.

THE PROBLEM My plans include only things that must be taught. Some days I have to cram in more than I should to make sure I cover the curriculum material. I don't think that's good for my students.

THE SOLUTION Everything in my business plan was vital to growing a successful business; that is, until a law was changed, or a competitor came up with a better product. Prioritizing is difficult, but necessary. Keep your eye on the big picture.

Let's sum up:

1. You develop your quarterly plan remembering you are a salesperson who has something the customer really wants—education.
2. Look back at the annual elements and break them down quarterly. Analyze the potential differences on a quarter-by-quarter basis.
3. Then, break that down to weekly, and ultimately to your daily lesson plan. This method of planning gives you a definite track to run on.
4. The best tool to use for this planning is an electronic calendar because of its flexibility.

Know Your School

A school is a community where all sorts of people coexist for a common purpose. You also could say it is an enterprise whose purpose is to educate. When a new member enters the school, it can present either a daunting or an exciting experience for those entering. New teachers and new students come in anxious, fretful, and fearful of how they will fit in.

The more senior members, who have reached their comfort level, can help or hinder newcomers by their actions or inactions. However, the real burden of gaining acceptance and understanding the environment lies with the newcomer. The following consists of suggestions on how you can smooth out the transition from confused newcomer to comfortable insider and someday to senior member.

Survey Every Inch of the Grounds

Finally, you have graduated and have that wonderful teaching certificate and teaching contract. Or you have finally been accepted to a teaching position at the school in your system where you have always dreamed of teaching. The principal seemed really nice when she took you around the school. You hope she stays that way. Doesn't matter, you can handle anything now. You feel ready.

You teachers who have taught for a while, hang on, stay with me. You bought this book because you had begun to have doubts about your ability to teach or whether you really wanted to continue teaching. If you haven't already begun to sense new and invigorating ideas after reading the first three chapters, they will come. Try to remember your first days of teaching as you read on. It will come back. That spark you had at the start will return as a flame.

At some point, your principal gave you a tour of the school's facilities. Now ask yourself this question: Where would a student go to skip class? If that doesn't pique your curiosity, nothing will. Take a look at the dark areas semi-concealed behind locker bays. They could work, at least for a short hiding period. Look in places such as restrooms, locker rooms, and the cafeteria.

Next look inside all classrooms, especially those near your room. Students might choose to hide out right under your nose, so to speak, by staying in an empty classroom next to yours. If your school has a library with lots of freestanding bookcases, take a look all around the room. The bookcases could conceal a student or two, or maybe more, from some-one who looks in through the front door.

There also may be semi-concealed spots outside the build-ing near the corners of the building. Make notes of these observations for review when you have everyone's teaching schedule. Then you will know when teachers occupy the classrooms and library.

Survey Every Inch of the Grounds Again

This time, tour the school with the maintenance people. What they know can help—or hurt—you. These are the people who know how to keep you warm in the winter and cool (assuming the school has air conditioning) during the warmer months. They know the location of the weakest water lines, and keep your bathroom and lounge clean. They supply you with new light bulbs when necessary. They can make your life at school pleasant or not. They know the location of all the following in respect of the location of your room, and can escort you to them if necessary: principal's office, dean of students' office, counselor's office, registrar's office, vice principal's office, nurse's office, teacher's lounge, library, cafeteria, gym, weight room, boys' and girls' locker rooms, chapel, bathroom facilities for students and for teachers if separate, and all exterior locations on the school grounds.

THE PROBLEM My school has a new building. The heating and air conditioning are controlled by a computer. I have a thermostat on my wall and it has buttons for adjusting the temperature. No matter which button I push, the room just gets warmer.

THE SOLUTION Your custodian or building maintenance person will know how to adjust it, if indeed it can be. Some new systems are centrally controlled. Whatever you do, don't open a window. That blows the central controls out of the park. Find your custodian and share your problem with him.

Pick a Kid to Show You Where the Good Skip Places Are (Risky)

Here's what some new teachers have done: pick a student to take you around. This could work well, but it has its downside too. That student may not show you his or her favorite corner, and therefore you will get a slanted picture, Also, the student may interpret your request as a friendly overture and either express a concern to the principal or become too friendly, expecting the same in return.

Using a student has a certain amount of uncontrollable risk. If you're a first-year teacher, stick with the building custodian or maintenance person to show you around.

Befriend the Administrative Assistants (Wise)

Make it a point to get to know the office personnel. Obviously a small school may only have one person in the office, but most schools will have two or more. When you go to school on that first day of preparation, make it a point to introduce yourself even if the principal introduced you at an earlier date.

Ask the personnel their names and, as you do this, look closely at their faces. Take note of the color of their eyes and hair. Give each person a flower, or flowers, and ask them to repeat their names.

Give these people your full attention. Flatter them by asking for the spelling of their last names. Tell them it's because you want to make sure you get them right. Ask them to pronounce their names. Tell them again it's because you want to get it right. The office personnel know who has the most power and control, who wants it, and who most influences the principal. (Don't tell your principal this small, yet very valuable, secret.) Additionally, they can tell you where any major conflicts exist, and what, if any, coalitions the teachers have formed.

Make it a point to stop by the office every day and visit for a few minutes, or at least hail a happy "good morning" to the administrative assistants. Don't forget how busy they are in the mornings, and that you will need them sometime during the school year. There's an old adage that says you can get better results with honey than vinegar.

Befriend the Teachers, Your Colleagues (Wiser)

Eat lunch where the other teachers eat. Pack your lunch if you don't want to buy from the cafeteria. Leave your room and find the others and socialize. Most of the time you will find that they want to help you. They can tell you the nitty-gritty things, such as what time you really must arrive in the morning, and how late to stay. They will tell you where to get supplies, make copies, and find out who the teacher's union representative is in your school, if there is a union. The principal told you most of these things, but butterflies in a newcomer's stomach often interfere with his or her memory system.

The most important area where the teachers can help you is with knowing the students. Unless all your students are as new to the school as you, the teachers will know them. Your colleagues may offer advice. Take it. Don't be so proud as to be foolish. You may have a real potential troublemaker in one of your classes. Normally that student has made himself or herself well known around the campus. Often that person is a bully. (In Chapter 11, you'll learn about handling bullies.)

As you get to know your colleagues, remember that the teacher dropout rate is very high, which means many people aren't happy in the profession. As a result, some may convey an attitude of "gloom and doom." With your level of preparedness, you can just let that roll off your back. A nice smile and a head nod will suffice at first. When they see how happy and confident you are they will catch it, unless they are too far gone, in which case they should just go. The teaching profession doesn't need burned-out, disgruntled teachers to undermine the profession and ultimately hurt the educational intent. Never forget, you are making a major contribution to tomorrow's future by teaching our kids.

THE PROBLEM I just started at a new school. I've taught for more than ten years and wanted to teach at this school because it's my alma mater. The teachers here are difficult, to say the least. They complain about everything.

THE SOLUTION Although it isn't easy to ignore negativity if it surrounds you, you still must do so. Actually, the best way to deal with this problem is with your sunny attitude of loving the kids and your job.

Learn Building Safety—Fire, Tornado, and Earthquake Drills, and More

Start with your classroom. Take a look at the fire escape chart and then follow it to see where it leads. You really don't want to delay getting out of the building in the event of a fire. The same goes for tornadoes and for hurricanes. You will find that the location of shelter for high winds is quite different from that for a fire. Normally during a windstorm everyone will go to an inside space that's considered safe, as compared to going outside for fire. Again, ask the custodian or maintenance person to show you around. Ask to see all the nooks and crannies that you might not otherwise have occasion to see. Why do this? Wouldn't you like to know that, if you let Johnny go to the library to research the history of the emperor penguin, he actually can find that information there, and how long it should take him? The same thing goes for the restrooms. Unless you become familiar with the contents of the library, and its distance from your room; and the bathroom's distance from your room; and the potentials for childhood dalliance between those rooms and yours, you can't control Johnny, or any other student, at least not on this issue.

Think about other problems that can arise. Suppose there's a fire in the building. The fire alarm goes off and everyone, you think, evacuates the building. Suddenly the dean of students comes running over to you, shouting that Johnny is missing. You stand there dumbfounded and seized by the horrible thought that Johnny is still in a burning building.

You suddenly remember letting him go to the restroom over half an hour ago, and then you forgot about him. That sudden sinking feeling in your gut overwhelms you. You have lost a child who may be trapped in the burning building, or if old enough to drive, has left the school grounds altogether—not good. The maintenance people will know what to do during any crisis like this, but it's an experience you can do without.

Consider another example: If your building has more than one floor, traveling the stairs probably has specific rules, which the principal gave to you. The maintenance person can tell you how well those rules work and what you should do if they don't.

THE PROBLEM Taking time out to respond to a fire drill makes no sense to me. Our school building is classified as fireproof, and is only two years old.

THE SOLUTION Fire drills are required by the state. There really is no such thing as a fireproof building. It's true that some buildings have a fire-resistive rating, which means the building will resist supporting fire for a certain time, but after that, it will burn. You want to get the kids to safety and also save yourself.

Learn All About Your School's History, Traditions, and Rituals

Every school has a unique culture, developed through the interpersonal relationships of the teachers, students, administrators, and staff. These are there to stay and normally have become as much a part of the student development and school experience as is the teaching. What is the dominant course? The course that has the largest number of students enrolled is not necessarily the dominant one. The dominant course is the one to which the principal pays most attention. Sometimes the standardized tests will reflect this.

You also need to look at the club and sports teams. The number of participants and activities each has planned will illustrate their importance in the school.

How did the school get its name, and mascot, and what does the mascot represent? You want to know how long the

school has been in the existing facility, and where it resided before this one. If a private school, find out as much as you can about the benefactors and where the money comes from for the operations. If there is an ongoing fund drive, find out as much as you can; participate if possible.

Does the school have a spirit day, a clown day, a skip day, or a pajama day? What is expected from faculty and staff regarding attendance at school sporting events? What teams does the school have? What is the dominant sport, if any? Do the students take pride in their school? What are the teachers' attitudes toward school spirit? Do the teachers respect the principal, and do they feel empowered to do their best teaching? Is there an atmosphere of giving responsibility and ownership to both the teachers and students for accomplishing their tasks? What role do the standardized tests play in terms of teachers' attitudes? Generally speaking, do the teachers like the students and teaching? Is the curriculum student-centered? It should be. After all, the education of the students is what we're all about. Do the teachers use the Internet for a knowledge source? They should.

THE PROBLEM I recently started teaching at a private school. I had a student who was not working on assignments and also causing trouble in class. I sent him to the office one particularly difficult day and the principal chastised me for not handling the case myself. I later found out that the student's parents were among the largest benefactors of the school.

THE SOLUTION Learning as much as possible about the school's culture pays off. Private schools generally live day to day from the tuition charges. Their real money comes from donations. Although you should not "play favorites" when dealing with a student because of the family largesse, you must put on your sales cap and find ways to work out such problems on your own. You'll learn more about discipline in Chapter 11.

Memorize All Lunch Options and Bus Schedules

Whether you're changing schools or just entering the teaching profession, know that lunch and bus schedules rule the roost. Someone must get the students to and from your facility to teach them, and once there, must feed them. So, if it is decided the bus drivers cannot drive in the snow, you will get a snow day to stay home and relax. Well actually, if you call reading and grading papers "relaxing," then that defines a snow day for a teacher.

The school has to schedule lunches to fit into the class schedule, but lunches must begin between 11:00 A.M. and 12:45 P.M. That said, does it sound like the lunch times accommodate the class schedule? I don't think so. It really doesn't matter whether school starts on time or has a delay for whatever reason; the kids must be fed between 11 A.M. and 12:45 P.M. or some close variation of this. That means you also will eat sometime during those times. Just like the students, the teachers will not all eat at the same time. It really is very important that you get the timing down, so memorize the lunch and bus schedules. Figure out what flexibility you have to eat at different times, and then do it. The bus schedule determines which group of students comes in first and therefore must eat first, meaning their teachers will also eat at that time. The later ones simply come in for lunch in the later part of the lunch period. Alternating your times as best you can will give you the opportunity to get to know more teachers.

Teachers invariably talk about their students during lunch. That makes it a working lunch for you, but you will hear invaluable things about your students. Now don't go all postal on me and throw this book down in disgust because you really don't get a lunch break. Big deal!

I spent more than thirty-five years in corporate America and can't remember ever having a "free-time" lunch. Whether eating a sandwich at my desk and working or going to lunch with my boss or my peers or with a client, the business dominated the conversation. Think of it as a great learning experience. The older teachers have a wealth of knowledge and will share it willingly over lunch. You ask how I know that. I know that people love to talk about themselves. Everyone identifies with his or her job. Thus, talking about our jobs is the same as talking about ourselves. And, in my personal experience doing business all over this country and in Europe, that axiom always held true. Sometimes shutting people up presents a problem, but never opening them up.

Depending on the size of your school, the faculty can number from two (including you) to hundreds. In the latter case, you need to concentrate on learning all their names. Past yearbooks can help. Failing that, focus on people's faces while you're being introduced. Remember something that will bring the name back. Make sure you speak to each person at every opportunity, calling his or her name when you approach, and saying yours when you shake hands. If you've gotten the name wrong he or she will correct you, and in the future, that will serve as a reminder.

One final thing to remember about getting all those teachers' names is that our minds are basically associating machines. If you ask about the background or ancestry or origin of the name of someone you've just met, the answer will help you remember. If you can find something with which to associate a person's name, go for it.

Now, let's go over the guidelines for really getting to know your school:

1. Survey the grounds with the principal, maintenance person, and a student.
2. Never forget how valuable the school's administrative assistants are.
3. Connect with the other teachers. Don't isolate yourself.

4. Make sure you know your school's history and tradition.
5. Don't forget that the schedule is basically controlled by the lunch schedule, and the bus arrival time.

CHAPTER 5

Organize Thyself

You must first believe in yourself before you can help others to believe in themselves. During my senior year in high school, when I began to really worry about whether I could make it in college, one of my teachers told me that succeeding in college was 95 percent desire and 5 percent intelligence. Was she telling me I lacked the intelligence? No, no, not at all. She was telling me that I needed to believe in myself. I thought about that for some time. Then I went back to her and I asked, "How do I know when I can believe in myself?" She smiled and said, "When you're organized." "Am I organized?" I asked, now more doubtful than before.

She responded again with a friendly smile, saying, "Take a good look at yourself. You'll find the answer."

Needless to say, I was stunned. How did that help? After all, I thought I had taken several looks. But, at the young age of eighteen, I didn't feel qualified to make the proper determination. After my first two successful years in college I finally figured out how to tell.

I looked at what I had accomplished solely on my own. I had done very well in school, never missing an assignment and garnering respectable grades. How did I do that not having anyone to remind me to go to class or to do the homework? I was organized.

Organize thyself and you can accomplish magnificent things. Now that you teach, the most important thing you need to do is to get to know your students. That takes organization.

Master Thy Students: Forewarned Is Forearmed

Do you remember the previous discussion of a teacher being a salesperson? You can't succeed in sales without knowing your customer. Don't try to mold the customer to your product; in the long run, you will have no customers. Remember, don't assume that your students know why they are in your classroom. You need to motivate them to empower their learning abilities. I have been recognized by a national organization for exceptional performance in motivation and empowerment of today's youth because of my innovative and enthusiastic methods of getting results in the classroom. That's what teachers do—and you must start by getting to know your students.

Become a risk taker. When you hear of a new technique and it makes sense to you, try it. You won't know whether it works unless you try it. If you have built the kind of bond with your students whereby they trust and respect you, they will respect your methods. They will let you know if they don't work. You will both know if they do work.

I remember when I first started in the business world. At that time businesses were run with one of two philosophies of management. Some managers used autocratic and authoritative methods, often making them appear power-drunk. Those managers believed that people basically lacked the desire to work. That explained the management style. We called these X Type Managers.

The other theory of management held that people wanted to work and succeed to feel good about themselves.

That style of manager would assign tasks or ask for solutions to problems. Once this manager assigned something he or she would move on to other things, confident that the employees would accomplish it as requested. If the employee offered a solution to a problem, this manager would support that employee's attempt to apply the solution to see if it would work until either it did or it failed. These were called Y Type Managers.

The marketplace had few Y types because of the newness of that philosophy. Therefore, most managers ran the workplaces autocratically, experiencing little innovation and considerable employee morale problems, resulting in unionization. The X Type Managers caused psychological problems such as depression, suicide, heavy drinking, and so on. They felt no need to get to know their employees. The Y Type managed companies became highly successful. One of the most renowned during the early stages was General Motors Corporation.

If you believe students can't be trusted, they won't let you down. If you don't think they have the brains to learn the material you want to teach them, again, they won't let you down. You need to think like the Y Type Managers. You need to get to know your students well, and follow a few suggestions to help them learn.

THE PROBLEM I can't turn my back without my students becoming unruly. They throw things, shout at each other, and some continue mumbling under their breaths.

THE SOLUTION At the very beginning of the school year, you establish your control. It sounds like it may be too late for you this school year. Once control is lost it's very difficult to regain. Take a good look at yourself. Do you dress professionally? Do you act professionally? Do you respect the students? The establishment of mutual respect will eliminate the problem you described.

How to Read Between the Lines of Student Portfolios

Every school has certain core courses that the students must take to graduate. In the language arts department at my high school we start the students out in their freshman year writing essays and various other types of pieces. We set up a folder for each student and ask that they put their finished, graded papers in these folders, their portfolios. Each year the portfolios move along with the students to the next level. At the end of each year we ask them to review their portfolios and write an essay reflecting on how they feel their writing changed. By their senior year they have quite a number of essays to look at, and many of the students, once they reach the maturity level of an eighteen-year-old, see the significance of that portfolio and how they developed not only as a writer, but as a person.

At the beginning of each year, when the teachers move the portfolios to the student's next level, we read them. Doing this, you will learn a significant amount about your students' writing skills and where they need help. More important, because you may not have met these students before, the portfolios provide great insight into them as individuals.

Most teens use brutal honesty in their writing. They haven't yet developed the skill we adults like to refer to as finesse, or concealed deceit. There are abundant theories out there on this. One theory is that the part of the brain that realizes every action has a consequence has not yet developed.

The essays in the portfolios may include novel analyses or book reports as well as several other essays. At the beginning of each year, ask your students to write an essay reflecting on their life at that point in time. When reading these particular essays you may pay little attention to the grammar, preferring to listen to their choice of words. Another great tool is to have the juniors write a college application essay, which they will rewrite in their senior year. Tell these students that the person reading the essay has their grade transcript, their service record, and their extracurricular activity record. That means the essay needs to tell that reader who the student is in order to determine whether the student will fit in at the university. The students will really struggle with this one. Take away other things they could write about, leaving them with their feelings. Teens go through so many chemical changes in their bodies as they mature that most of the time they don't really know who they are. So, give them some help. Ask them to make a list of the people or things most important to them. After they have a minimum of twenty minutes to work on this, call the students up to your desk one at a time. Look at each list, hand it back, and ask the student to indicate the most important. Then ask for the second, and third, and so on.

Almost without exception, the first choice the students originally listed was the most important to them. Obviously, it came to their conscious mind first and they wrote it down. The second on the list is nearly always second. From the third item on, some variations begin to develop, but not many. Finally, tell each student to go back and write their essay, and make sure the receiver knows their priorities as they selected them.

Many of them look at their lists with astonishment. They had never before had to prioritize their value system. Doing this exercise seems to bring comfort to them in knowing a little more about themselves. You benefit by getting to see inside their heads with clarity. You may never have gotten that insight any other way. Their portfolios will do nearly the same thing for you. When essays first mention parents, and next their siblings and God, you can bet you have a kid who's good down deep. Because of the many nuances in personality, another benefit of the college essay is learning a student's secret ambitions, or possibly even that some are thinking of harming themselves because of depression.

What does all this information do for teaching and classroom management? It allows you to understand the students much better without prying, and to learn their priorities and other things that add to your ability to interact with them. You can have an interesting discussion with them about what they want to do with their lives.

If you asked most adults who they are, you would probably get a blank stare. But if you asked them what they do, they would answer with their job classification, such as lawyer or plumber or nurse. Tell these young adults that what you see is a person, not an occupation. Tell them we never become our work, no matter how hard we work at it. Each of us becomes a man or a woman who has the capacity to love, work, and play. Our work has a huge influence on how we view life, but we do not become our work. For example, I know a lawyer who specializes in title work for real estate, another one who specializes in handling workers' compensation claims, several who specialize in tort liability, and others who, although involved in tort liability, only get involved with insurance cases. The title lawyer, on his second marriage after having a first marriage destroyed by a philandering spouse, seems to have found happiness. The lawyer who specializes in workers' compensation claims is married with a couple of kids, and seems like a solid citizen—until you take a closer look at exactly what he does for a living. Without going into too much detail, let's just say he's a parasite on society who does unconscionable things to get clients. One of the tort lawyers has a great marriage, works in church activities, and makes a fortune getting involved in convoluted tort cases.

If you asked any one of these individuals who they are, they would quickly say "a lawyer." But, as I have briefly demonstrated, they are really very different people. What has that got to do with teaching? When you discuss the college application essays with the kids, stress they are already the person they want to become when they grow up, just in the early stages. Why tell them that? Because kids, and teens in particular, tend to label each other, and a job title is just another label. It's what's in their minds and hearts that's important, not what they will see in their paycheck.

When reading their portfolios, look for indications showing whether the student knows, or has some idea of, who he or she is. Look for active words and phrases such as "interested in engineering," "love my brothers and sisters," "want to be," "like," "love," "then I knew," "cannot find a reason for being here" (meaning being here in this world—this phrase is a very red flag).

Another way to get to know students is to listen in on their conversations. Teens in particular are so self-centered that you can be sitting at the desk next to them while they discuss how much they hate another student or teacher or coach, and they'll never skip a beat.

THE PROBLEM I always keep my ears open and sometimes wish I hadn't. I don't know if they are teasing or serious and may be talking about hurting someone.

THE SOLUTION Err on the side of caution. Report the conversation to your principal.

Ask for Input from Colleagues and Office Personnel

Never hesitate to ask another teacher about a student. You can expect a straightforward, helpful answer. As a matter of fact, in all my many years of working I have never worked with a group of people who cared more about the results of their work than do teachers. So don't be shy.

The time will come when you must consult with either the principal or dean of students, or counselor, or vice principal—whoever handles such matters. Those times come about when you hear a student threaten someone or threaten to harm himself or herself. If you have your students keep journals, you must tell them that you will read what they write, and that if you read anything that sounds like they may harm themselves or another person, you have to report it to the school authorities. A journal can be a pamphlet or binder or folder where the student files personal comments written in your class. For example, creative writing students often write in a journal on a regular basis to get practice in free writing, and as a good stimulus for the creative muse. When the students finish writing on any given day, they should place their journals in a cabinet that you keep locked. They know that you are the only person other than themselves who will see it.

I had one instance where a student wrote beautiful but very dark poetry in her journal. I studied it very carefully before discussing it with her. I told her some of it sounded suicidal. She did not say a word, but gave me that how-did-you-know look only a teenager can give. When I told her I had to report my suspicions she just nodded, again without saying anything. Writing those poems in a journal she knew I would read was, to me, a cry for help. I had to seek consultation with my principal in that case.

Pay attention to the students' classroom attitude, completion of assignments, participation in class projects, and how they communicate and react to each other. If a bright student who ordinarily does assignments well and on time, and always has his or her hand up to participate suddenly turns quiet, or even sullen, and is not responding or doing assignments, ask if everything is okay. Call the parents, talk to the guidance counselor or principal, ask other teachers, and complete and turn in any form your school provides for a teacher who becomes concerned about a student.

All of these changes in student behavior potentially point toward drug abuse at some level, but also could indicate onset of an illness. You must do as much as you can to get at the problem and get it in front of someone who can take care of it as soon as possible.

One final comment on asking for input from colleagues has to do with a teacher mentor program for first-year teachers. Most schools do this. Your principal will assign an experienced teacher and very likely will require you to meet with this person regularly during your first year. Your administration does not do this as an intrusion or an insult to your level of knowledge or professionalism. You will need help from an experienced person, but your shyness may cause reluctance to ask. The mentor program takes care of that issue.

Master the Clock and Bell and Block Schedule

There is documented evidence that the years of slavish adherence to the forty-two-minute class period became a major factor in the demoralization of teachers and students. It wasn't until the early 1990s that at least one school's principal began to realize two things: forty-two-minute class times prevented getting into anything in any depth, and because of this, both students and teachers became clock-watchers.

In turn, those clock-watching students scored poorly on standardized tests. They couldn't focus on the subject matter, frustrating teachers who knew they couldn't do the job they wanted to do.

Max Alexander's story in the May 2006 *Reader's Digest Special Issue* reports that in 1992 a new principal came into an Ohio high school that used the regular forty-two-minute periods. The school's ninth-grade students had low passing percentages on standardized tests—50 percent on the state's math proficiency test, and 69 percent in reading. Only 8 percent earned honors diplomas. One of the first things the new principal did was to begin grilling students for ideas on how to improve their test scores. He also visited other schools and attended seminars whenever he became aware of a new program, and held intensive meetings with his teaching staff. He instituted the following changes:

- He replaced the forty-two-minute class and credit-hour system with eighty-minute blocks.
- He created student portfolios by subject, which allowed the students to see their development in each subject. These portfolios included essays from English class, research papers from science, math problems based on level of difficulty, papers written in the foreign language they studied, essays on historical events, and so on. Alternatively, he permitted one consolidated portfolio per student, with dividers set up for each subject. The portfolios were set up in the freshman year so that students, parents, and teachers could track student development throughout high school.
- He and his staff developed practical courses such as tractor repair and student group development of recipe books. Core courses required everyone to read Shakespeare, Emerson, and Thoreau.
- He eliminated clocks from the classrooms.
- He replaced the daily, short homeroom period used for announcements and attendance with a once-a-week advisory meeting. Each teacher advises the same group of students all the way through their high school careers.
- He extended the lunch period from twenty minutes to an hour to give the students time to study.

During the first four years of this program, the students' passing percentages on the Ohio math proficiency test scores went from 50 percent to 85 percent; passing grades in reading went from 69 percent to 96 percent; and honors diplomas increased from 8 percent to 20 percent. Even though the principal says the school didn't focus on test scores, it became clear that paying attention to the overall culture of the school would result in higher test scores. Allowing the students the opportunity to work on something they had an interest in, such as tractor repair in this rural area, caused them to want to study the core courses in more depth, resulting in the higher test scores.

There are many other case studies of schools that set up teacher teams or advisers to counsel small groups of teens, either throughout their high school careers or for two of their four years at the school, thus building valuable bonds with the students. Others have added non-textbook literature and hands-on lab work and field trips, resulting in higher passing percentages on state-mandated tests.

THE PROBLEM If we take the clocks out of our classrooms once students have become accustomed to having them, they will scream.

THE SOLUTION Communication is the key to effective change. Announce well in advance the elimination of clocks from your room. Remind your students twice, several days apart, and then remove the clocks. Many kids will still ask where the clock went. Once you explain the concept of the freedom from time, they will stop questioning and accept the concept of no clocks.

Master Thyself: Take Time to Prepare

In order for you to become a good, well-organized teacher in control of your classroom, you must first figure out who you really are.

If you have just graduated from college and have yet to develop a routine for yourself, you have no sins, so to speak, of which to rid yourself. You have the opportunity to come out of the blocks with a full steam of energy fueled by enthusiasm. If you've taught for a while and feel burned out, you probably have forgotten about taking care of yourself. We all have an inherent need to organize ourselves. At the core of a happy person is organization in their life. You don't have to go off the deep end and become an obsessive-compulsive personality. You simply need to take prep time for yourself, to think, review, and rehearse for opening day. By writing out your strategy for the first day of school and rehearsing it, you will present the picture of a self-confident professional, because your mind will have absorbed the list of points you want to mention.

Bring your notes with you on that first day. You will feel confident and may even get through the list you made. Don't concern yourself if you don't, because that will just mean that more important things came up. Here are topics to put on your list:

- Welcome—state name—identify room—subject
- Introduce myself—background—how I came to teaching—some books I like to read
- Describe topics of study—activities—sample projects—textbook
- Classroom rules—ask your administrator for student rules
- Syllabus
- A quick lesson
- If time, go around and shake hands and ask each student to introduce himself or herself to you.

"Training is everything. The peach was once a bitter almond: cauliflower is nothing but cabbage with a college education."
                                    —Samuel L. Clemens (Mark Twain)

You must prepare for your opening-day speech as though you are a president-elect preparing for your inaugural address to the nation. By now, whether knowingly or unknowingly, you have selected a method of memorization, and it may very well work for you when taking tests. But, when speaking on that first day, you must impress a new group of students with your knowledge, sincerity, and realness. If you actually memorize and repeat your talk verbatim, it will sound stilted and disingenuous.

For many years now I have believed in the "blab school" of remembering a speech because it applies to the importance of that opening day. It seems that President Abraham Lincoln attended one of those one-room schoolhouses where children of all ages learned together. The school had only one textbook, so the teacher read it aloud to the class and the students repeated it, all of them at once. The neighbors, upon hearing this uproar every day, dubbed the school the "blab school." Throughout his life, when Lincoln wanted to remember something, he would read it out loud.

When the commission in charge of the Gettysburg cemetery decided to arrange for a formal dedication they invited Lincoln, who, to their surprise, agreed to come. Lincoln brooded over his speech for several days, and rewrote it several times. He called this process of rereading and rewriting giving it "another lick." The night before he was to deliver this important speech, he read it aloud to his Secretary of State, William H. Seward, asking for, and receiving, criticism. Lincoln breakfasted early the next morning to continue giving it "another lick" until the announcement came for him to depart for the ceremony. Many have said he continued to brood over it until he arrived at the cemetery, where he delivered one of the most memorable, albeit brief, speeches in our nation's history: The Gettysburg Address.

Why write about Lincoln in a book on teaching? What better example of preparation and passion could there be? This first day sets the stage for your teaching for the rest of the year. The impression you give on that day will last a very long time, and you will have great difficulty overcoming a failure.

Once past that first day, make sure you properly utilize your planning periods to prepare classes, review subject material and any outside material you want to use, and think about how your classes will go. Visualize the classroom filled with students. Using this time well takes such a high priority that it is the subject of the next chapter.

THE PROBLEM I freeze when I have to give a formal speech. I do all right in the classroom unless a topic demands a lecture. I much prefer hands-on instruction.

THE SOLUTION The reason you do all right in the classroom is because you know your subject. The ideas or concepts are deeply imbedded rather than a recalling of specific words in a specific order. Apply this same approach to a speech or lecture. Don't attempt to memorize the exact words. Just learn the ideas.

Before going on, let's go over what you've learned in this chapter:

1. You must believe in yourself before you can believe in anyone else.
2. If you believe your students are dummies who don't want to learn, they won't let you down. You must have faith in their abilities and recognize it is your job to bring out their strong points.
3. Use every available tool to understand your students. The portfolio works very well. You must then learn how to interpret what students say in their writings. If you're new to this profession, ask for help anywhere you can get it. Your fellow teachers hold a wealth of information. Listen to them. Confide in them.
4. Prepare yourself for opening day. You only get one chance at making that all-important first impression.
5. Master time or it will master you.
6. Make sure you use your planning periods to review what you've taught so you know where to go.
7. Think and review constantly.

The Beginning: A Good Teacher Is Very, Very Good on Opening Day

CHAPTER 6

Prep Time at Your School

If you wanted to succeed in a business, you wouldn't start it without proper preparation. Similarly, you won't succeed at the daily task of teaching without proper preparation, above and beyond the planning discussed in the first part of this book. Don't think that once you've finished your initial planning, you can simply walk into that classroom and teach successfully.

You will have periods of down time during your day. You must use them to review and prepare. Whether you have the traditional forty-two-minute classes or block scheduling, your schedule should include a planning period. Use it wisely.

Why This Time Is Critical for You and Your Students

During your school day you will have a period or two for preparation. Take full advantage of this time by doing the following:

■ **Take a deep breath.** Sit back and relax completely. Allow your arms to fall gently to your sides. Exhale slowly and feel the tension flow out of your body. Close your eyes and visualize that sunny beach you walked last summer, or the flowers in your garden you so admire. Now you're ready to take full advantage of your planning period.

- **Review your class lecture recordings.** I have an Olympus Digital Voice Recorder that works well for this purpose because it automatically goes into sleep mode after only two seconds of silence, and starts right up again when you speak. It can record continuously up to four hours, so I don't have to stop a class or a lecture to change anything. If you decide to use a device like this, make sure you transfer the recordings onto a CD or to another computer. That way you prevent the recorder from filling up and stopping on you, and in the awful event of it crashing and losing the information, you will have it elsewhere. You will also want to have this information for an absent student.

- **Review your plan to compare your expectations to actual events.** Remember, we don't learn by a steady acceleration, like driving your car away from a stop light. Most of our learning is by fits and starts. Make adjustments to your daily plan to accommodate this.

- **Prepare new quizzes or tests rather than always using previous ones, and make copies.** Later you will learn about computerizing these.

- **Grade papers and record grades.** Review your grading scheme to make sure it does what you want it to do.

- **Read material that you will use in the next class.** This will keep your approach fresh and enthusiastic.

- **Although this may seem like a good time to talk to parents, you must ration your planning periods carefully for the sake of expediency and your long-term sanity.** You need most of this period for class preparation, which is similar to what you did for opening day preparation, only now more in-depth in the subject matter. I prefer to call parents after my last class to steer clear of my planning period. I had 120 students last year and used about ten minutes of my daily planning time for receiving phone calls or e-mails.

- **Think about your next class** and visualize the kids as though you and they were there.

- **Practice any new lectures you have written.** Say them out loud so that you will hear grammatical errors or difficult phrasing that will cause you to stumble.
- **Guard this personal time carefully short of excluding all outside factors.** If a student has an emergency and wants your help, you must give it.

Sometime during the day in most high schools, the students will have study halls or free periods. Some will most likely misuse this time by sleeping or talking with their friends. If the principal asks you to monitor one of these during your preparation period, you must comply. Unfortunately, this can dramatically reduce your free time. You may want to request relief from this monitoring chore if you can do so without risking insubordination. You really need your planning time, and monitoring a study hall can be like baby-sitting. In any event, do your best to impress on the students in these classes the importance of good time management, which can save them from having so much homework every evening. You must persist in keeping them quiet enough to study, or at least to read and think (a little bit, anyway), because many of them view study halls as social events. Obviously planning times in primary grades will not include study halls.

All of you must make time for planning every day, even if it's not in your official schedule. Coming in early helps prepare the day. Staying over as long as it takes to review the day and make the adjustments you need for the next day is a good use of your time. You also need to remember that you do not operate in a vacuum. Other teachers in your school go through the same things, and periodically, normally once a month, your principal will have in-service meetings to get you all together.

THE PROBLEM I just can't get my lesson plans adjusted to accommodate the student learning rates.

THE SOLUTION Don't forget flexibility. Come in an hour early and stay an later hour. That time will allow you to make your adjustments. Also, try a computerized calendar for recording your plans (see Chapter 3).

Making the Most of In-Service Meetings

Can you hear the grumbling? "I don't have time for this!" "We never do anything useful!" "She asks for our vote on something and then ignores it!"

Speaking of ignoring something, ignore those comments. You say your principal has gotten into a rut and really doesn't pay any attention to voting for issues. Don't concern yourself with that either. Why? Because it only takes one thinker willing to express his or her thoughts at one of these meetings to eventually change the atmosphere. Remember the infectious nature of enthusiasm.

Don't get carried away asking useless questions that sound like time killers. I have never had much patience for those kinds of questions or the people who ask them. Ask questions of substance, questions that have to do with your own goals and the school's overall goals.

You new teachers, who may be shy about asking questions, just listen. Pay attention to the persons asking questions and the questions they ask. You will learn a lot about your fellow teachers and their priorities as well as benefit from the answers received.

Suppose questions come up regarding discipline. (That very likely will top the list in most schools.) The questions will tell you a lot about the questioners, as well as provide guidelines for discipline.

We always have to be wary of the "opposiphobes," or the people who not only disagree with everything, but think they have the right answer for everything. Ever run into those? No matter what you think, they will have a "better" idea, and listening to them can be very depressing. Try to sort through their rhetoric, though, because even they occasionally have good ideas. Don't worry about who they are. After a meeting or two, or some lunchroom discussion, you'll know them.

Back to the discipline question. The question asked by one of these people can tell you that the questioner has lost control of his or her classroom. It can also generate comments from other teachers that will help you in your classroom. Therein lies one of the potential benefits of in-service meetings. Many principals use them to introduce new teaching concepts, or make you aware of a problem that is occurring in the school.

I remember one meeting where the dean of students announced that kids were asking for permission to go to the restroom about halfway through the last period. They may or may not have gone to the restroom, but they did leave the campus without returning. As I thought about that I remembered that I had allowed one of my students to go to the restroom at such a time. Because I had so engrossed myself in the class, I forgot about him. He didn't return to class that day.

That may not sound like a big deal except for the fact that we must accept the responsibility for knowing the location of our students at all times. They could leave the campus and get hurt, do drugs, have sex, and on and on. Guess what the parents would do about that.

In-service meetings offer many opportunities to learn details about teaching that may not otherwise have occurred to you. These will be discussed later. Just keep that positive attitude toward these meetings. Set your sights to see the possibilities of new teaching methods, and try them.

THE PROBLEM I hate going to in-service meetings. We have a couple of teachers on our staff who seem to use that time as a gripe session.

THE SOLUTION Obviously, you can't completely control them. Pay close attention to the topics of discussion and when comments begin to get off the track, raise your hand and politely, even meekly, ask the principal the subject of the previous topic on the agenda. Say that you aren't sure if you understood it. Believe it or not, the interrupters will eventually get the message.

Practice Makes Perfect

Can you believe that this actually applies to the teaching profession? Of course it does, and in more ways than one. Yet, we have to take care that practice doesn't make boring. With three junior English classes myself, it can be very hard to keep them all at the same level of development. Doing so means repetition of lectures and quizzes, and on and on. So, then, just what does "practice makes perfect" mean for you?

How many times have you said something during your lectures in the second or third class on the same subject and wondered if you had already taught that in that class? In actuality you were teaching it for the first time to each of those classes. You vets out there—does that ever happen to you? What you just said sounded so much like you had just said it a minute ago, that you pause and wonder if the kids were being polite by not saying anything, or didn't care if you repeated it (after all, every word you said used up class time).

Not only do you say the same thing in each class, but the time you spent preparing meant you had thought through and said almost the exact same thing then, but just for practice of course. Yes—practice.

Think of yourself as one of the great public speakers. Study the careers of great speakers and you will find that they all practiced over and over. They also learned that the best form of practice occurs when you allow time lapses during practices so the subconscious mind can go to work on it, making the associations needed for long-term memory. Allowing the time lapses also does not fatigue the mind as much as does hour upon hour of forced information. So to attempt to memorize something within a short time of its delivery can result in the disaster of memory lapse. How much do you remember from those college exam cram sessions?

It's Gotta Matter

Enthusiasm, passion, and desire form the basis for having something you want to say. Without these, no conviction, no zeal, and no impetus will motivate your expression. You will fall flat.

Recently my students delivered assigned speeches in my classroom. We spent two class periods while everyone had their turn. Each student gave a speech based on a topic he or she picked from a list compiled based on what I knew about their interests. I created a grid with speaking requirements on it such as eye contact, voice inflection, and so on. Each student graded the other students using these same criteria by using the grid sheets. Many gave their speeches to get it over with. The students diligently graded them accordingly. Many covered their subject in phenomenal detail given the four-minute time constraint. Some spoke clearly, enunciating their words with perfection. But when one particular student got up to speak, stood at the podium, and gave an almost evil look around the room before even beginning to speak, I knew something special was about to happen. He didn't disappoint us. He began in a near whisper, as we leaned in to hear. His voice built to a near crescendo that would have rivaled the greatest of the world's operatic tenors, and no one was taking notes on their grids. Then he stopped. He had finished on time and subject. He paused for a moment, again looking around the room with his serious stare, and walked to his seat. The pens flew, making notes. He had us.

Upon reviewing the speech paper he had given me, I noticed it had only four points written on it. He also hadn't actually said a lot because he spoke slowly, as though each word held extreme importance. He didn't go into any sort of intricate detail on his topic. What, then, had us? He had enthusiasm, passion, conviction, and the desire to motivate us to accept his idea, because he knew without a doubt not only the importance it held for him, but for us. He didn't need a lot of words. His facial expressions reflected an earnest bearing and attitude. He could have been selling his fellow students on increasing the school day by double, and they would have bought it.

Think of some ways you can perform like that student. Start with the surroundings.

THE PROBLEM No matter how I read poetry to my students, they either fall asleep or zone out.

THE SOLUTION Obviously, your enthusiasm is lacking. You need to love it for them to appreciate it. Find a local poetry reading group and listen in. Have a teacher who doesn't like poetry read a poem to you. Consider your feelings while listening to both sources. You have to love it.

Organize That Classroom

Earlier, there was an example of the classroom teacher standing at his or her podium in front of a room full of bored students. You can easily picture that in your mind. I can relate to that from a comment one of my students made to another when he didn't think I could overhear.

We were studying poetry and poetic technique, so I asked them to write a poem. Knowing the difficulty of that task for most students, I put them in pairs so they could bounce their poems off someone. While walking around the room to see how they were doing, I overheard a student saying "I hate this stuff!"

How could I get this student to at least soften his attitude? Surely the class had others who felt the same. Wow, that presented an even greater challenge than did getting them to like poetry. I wouldn't have heard the comment if the student hadn't made it while I stood so near. That was when I came up with arranging the students' desks in a V shape.

Some of the other teachers started doing something similar. One used a complete circle, but that seemed to best lend itself to the smaller classes. Others had desks lined along the walls to the teacher's right and left, the desks faced inward toward the center of the room. This usually required the desks to be three or four deep, and left an aisle down the center of the room where the teacher could walk back and forth. That was still not good enough to hear them.

Students need to be no more than two desks away from you. A V-shaped open space in the center of the room does the trick. The first row of desks in the V has six on a side; the second has seven. That takes care of twenty-eight students, none of which are more than two desks away from you. I have a couple of classes with thirty students, so I have had to move everyone closer to accommodate them. Here's an axiom to live by—the closer the speaker, the more attentive the listener.

Have you ever attended a speaking engagement and had the speaker walk down the aisles as he spoke? In addition, did he or she make comments that had personal meaning for the folks nearest the speaker? I have, and that certainly left a great impression. That speaker held us in his hands for three of the shortest hours I can remember. He never stopped moving. He could always be heard, even when he was in the back of the room. And he had that same thing that my speech student had. Enthusiasm.

It is very difficult to fall asleep or let your mind wander if the person speaking to you is right in front of you. And if the speaker has something to say that you want, or need, to know, you will follow that person wherever he or she goes. It takes a lot of practice for a public speaker to master that skill. As a matter of fact, at the end of his presentation, the speaker I just told you about introduced one of his staff, who was standing at the rear of the room; another, who was standing to the right; and another, who stood to the left. He made sure we could hear him at all times by watching for their signals if his voice dropped too much.

THE PROBLEM I have thirty-one freshmen in my classroom. The school is old and the room was designed for twenty-five students with their desks lined up in five rows of five each. I tried placing the rows closer, with seven rows of five in a row, but that had the kids so close together it made it easier for them to cheat on tests, so cheat they did, and I had to reprimand several of them several times. I can't think of any other way to place the desks so I can be closer to them, so they stay awake during the class, and so they are less inclined to cheat. I have my desk up front so I can watch them better.

THE SOLUTION Obviously, you have too many kids for the space. There are two things you can do. First of all, move your desk to the rear of the room, and you will still be able to watch them, but they won't be able to know when you are looking at them. This will reduce the cheating. Second, place the desks in a V pattern, with three rows of ten and one desk either out in front and facing the others or, in the back next to your desk. Walk around the V while lecturing. Also walk around the V during testing, alternating with walking in the back. With the V shape you can see their desks better, and your closeness will discourage sleepiness during your lectures.

Can we all be that good? Probably not in a public setting, but most assuredly we can in our classroom. Organize those desks to support your best delivery. Follow this list and you'll have them where you want them:

1. Determine the attitude of the class toward what you have to say. You may teach the same subject to four different classes if you have block scheduling, or as many as eight if not. Each class has its own dynamic, which will require a different approach to get and hold the students' attention.

2. Humor is good. Seriousness is good. But to overdo either can reduce the effect of your message. True conviction of your message will make for an automatic blending of these.

3. Most people lack the ability to express enthusiasm to the point of it becoming contagious, so expect it to take work.

4. Remember that your message is important. Your students need what you have to offer.

5. Do not memorize your lectures verbatim. Burn the real important elements of your subject into your mind.

6. The facts you impart are important, but don't forget to display what's in your heart.

7. The big thing in lecturing is not the words spoken, but your spirit behind those words.

8. Stand tall, use enthusiastic gestures, and look straight at the students. Your eyes will pull them in.

9. Don't use weak words such as "seem," or "I think," or "possibly," as these will leave them flat, wondering just what you really mean.

10. Love your students.

CHAPTER 7

Getting Their Attention—From Day One

Your Appearance

What does it mean when someone comments about the importance of your appearance as a teacher? Don't they care that you've spent several years and a lot of hard work studying to learn how to teach? So what if you come to school on Monday with your hair askew and a day's growth of beard after a rough weekend when your fiancée broke off the engagement? Blue jeans make you feel comfortable and help you actually express yourself. Why doesn't your principal want you to wear them? You actually like spiked hair. Why not fix it that way, when you go shopping at the mall? Anyway, what does it mean to dress properly? The kids have chains, pants down around their knees, and bling all over their ears. Why can't you do that if you like it?

Many of you, especially recent college graduates, hold the opinion that people should not judge you by what you wear. I couldn't agree more. In theory, we should not judge anyone by the clothes they wear. But, the reality still remains—we do.

Dress for Success

How do you, a teacher, dress for success? There is certainly more than one school of thought on that. This problem didn't exist when I worked as an executive and business owner. Although the standard dress for men evolved from dark suits, white starched shirts, black highly polished shoes, and a maroon or navy blue or black tie in the 1960s and '70s to casual dress suitable for playing a round of golf in the 1980s and '90s, we always knew what appropriate clothing to wear.

Unfortunately, for the ladies, wearing the right apparel has always presented complications. Until the casual '80s and '90s, and the final breaking of the glass ceiling in the '90s and the new millennium, women who worked in business offices were told that they should wear non-revealing blouses and skirts and a modicum of makeup with clean, nicely styled hair, and well-polished flats or pumps with heels no higher than two inches.

Once women broke through the infamous glass ceiling and became management, knowing the proper attire became more complicated. Should they wear dark, pin-striped suits and starched white blouses, assuming that "manly" look? Or would they do better in their career to wear more frilly clothing, reflecting a more feminine persona? The financial businesses always had a conservative reputation that carried over to their employees' dress, and that simplified the apparel question for everyone working in those fields.

But what about you, the teachers of high school and elementary schoolchildren today? Will what you wear really matter to the children you teach? It may seem, on the surface, that what you wear has no influence, but rest assured that it does. Try to wear something totally out of character, and the kids will jump all over you with questions.

There are two major schools of thought on the subject of teachers' appearance. The first theory says we should dress casually and well, similar to the better-dressed teens in the local high school. The kids will then see us as adults with whom they can connect. The other says to dress like a corporate executive, with starched button down shirts and slacks for men and blouses paired with long skirts or dress pants for women.

Do I have a recommendation? Absolutely! Dress for respect. Whether you teach adolescents or teens, not only do they not want nor expect you to dress like them, they will not respect you if you do. You need to dress like a professional in order to be treated like a professional. It does not matter whether you go for the corporate pinstriped suit or casual pleated khakis, make sure everything you wear is of good quality—no holes or rips—and well pressed.

THE PROBLEM I simply can't afford good clothes.

THE SOLUTION Have you tried Goodwill stores, or St. Vincent DePaul Thrift stores? Some cities have consignment stores or secondhand stores that feature gently used, but stylish clothes. Swallow your pride and try these sources. The clothes won't be the latest style, but they will be affordable.

Ladies, dress as well as you can afford, remembering not to wear jeans. You don't have to wear cutting-edge fashion. Just never, never reveal too much flesh or wear anything too tight, especially cleavage when around teenage boys. Gents should wear business suits or blazers with well-pressed slacks, and a starched shirt with contemporary tie. Oh, and a two-day growth of beard may work for Brad Pitt and be popular among the teens, but it's not for you.

Don't forget that you teach impressionable young people even when you go out shopping, dancing, or just relaxing. You should never forget decorum and modesty. The one thing a young person definitely doesn't need is a mixed message.

Another dress issue has to do with spirit days. An explanation for the uninitiated: Many schools designate one day a week to drum up support for the school sports teams and other extracurricular activities. Many hold pep rallies, while others have special gatherings with the athletes to interview them and discuss the upcoming game. Still others have their marching band march through the halls of the school playing the school fight song. Most schools recommend wearing school sweatshirts and dress pants. So what do you wear on those days? You can wear one of the school T-shirts with a clean, pressed pair of slacks, or a school shirt or golf shirt with dress pants, slacks, or a skirt. Suppose, in spite of this recommendation, you choose to dress down to a sweatshirt, jeans, and running shoes on one of those occasions. First of all, make certain the principal approves before dressing down to the casual mode. Even if the principal does approve, I still do not advise it. Some of your students, subconsciously at least, will think you want to be one of them and may treat you as such. Imagine that you are walking down a hallway, dressed in your sweatshirt, jeans, and running shoes, and one of those unthinking teens slaps you on the back and greets you by your first name or a nickname. You suddenly have a problem. Remember, it's okay to be friendly, but not a friend.

THE PROBLEM All the teachers in my school wear jeans. We have a serious respect problem and it undermines our ability to teach. Is there a connection between the jeans and the lack of respect?

THE SOLUTION Yes. Although your principal allows jeans, you should wear dress pants if male or skirt if female. Also wear a dressy shirt and tie or a neat blouse. Your professional look will catch on, and the respect issue will fade away in time.

Your Attitude

As you'd expect, your attitude makes a big difference in how you are perceived. Here are some dos and don'ts.

Dos: PMA, Accountability, Mutual Respect, Humor

PMA (Professional Mental Attitude) simply means never forget your position and its influence. If your students think of you first as one whom they rely on for good advice, then you have succeeded. Even though I teach English, more than one student has stopped me in the hall and asked how to solve an algebra problem, or some other problem that I have no idea how to solve. The student was making a sincere request because he or she saw me as a teacher. In the case of the algebra problem, I told the student my knowledge of algebra had long since left me, but I knew where he could get help. I quickly led him to the library, where an algebra teacher monitored a study group.

As a teacher you have not only accountability for providing instruction in your field of expertise, but for acting as a member of the total teaching staff at your school. Always remember that, and always maintain a good sense of humor. These may very well be the most important axioms in this book.

Don'ts: Pomposity, Pomposity, Pomposity

Do not get in the habit of giving curt or smart-aleck answers to students outside the classroom. Adolescents and teens have the ability to say or do all the wrong things at all the wrong times, even to the point of sounding comically stupid to you and, therefore, deserving of short or curt answers and your naturally quick wit. The student won't get it. Your words are not wasted; they are destructive. If you can't give a good, honest response, rather than curtness; if you don't know the answer, or understand the question, say so. That really doesn't show a lack of professionalism. You don't have to know everything. Listen carefully so you really understand what they want before responding. School should present the forum for intelligence-gathering, so assume that's what the student is doing.

Your Rules

Let's take a more in-depth look at rules and how they'll affect your teaching.

School Rules

Some of these were introduced in Chapter 2. We now need to take a more in-depth look at them. A society, a school, cannot function without order, and order results from rules. Every school will, therefore, have variations on a set of rules or guidelines. Inner-city schools concerned about kids bringing guns and knives onto the premises or into schools will have rules reflecting that concern, and their rules will most certainly differ from those of a school in a small town where lower-middle-class working people make up the majority of the town's population. The rules of a private school drawing students from an upper-middle to upper-class community will differ from private, religion-based schools, even though it draws students from the same community and income level.

The first rule of learning the school rules, then, has to do with understanding both the community at large and the type of school. Study the demographics of the area for income levels, types of work, religions, crime types and ethnic groups. Once you do that—and it shouldn't take but a few hours on the Internet and a conversation with one of the teachers who grew up in the area—you will know the basis for the school rules. Then you can be more assured of applying the right level of importance to each.

Next, discuss with the principal the demographics of the student body. Get to know your students and their parents as well as possible. Throughout this book you will find mention of the different ways to get to know the students, their families, and their goals. All this sets the stage for creating viable classroom rules based on mutual respect.

Classroom Rules

The following examples form the basis for classroom rules and assume knowledge of the school rules:

- **Major offenses include anything that disrupts the flow of learning.** Specific behaviors come to my mind, but what's most important is that your values determine the rules that fit you and your students. It doesn't matter which course you're teaching; it's the learning environment that matters most. Many of the behaviors that warrant this level of offense fall into the category of rudeness. What is rudeness? For the sake of clarity, here are some examples: talking when either you or another student was already talking; getting out of their seats without permission; taking the Lord's name in vain, or using vulgar language; throwing anything; leaving a cell phone turned on, allowing it to ring; committing vulgar actions such as rubbing their groin that are subject to your interpretation, not theirs; using foul slang that they know you won't understand; taking notes or talking or sleeping or doing anything except listening when you read or say the meditation at the beginning of class.

- **Lesser offenses fall into the category of behaviors that are irritating but do not necessarily disrupt the class.** You must allow for the possibility of a reasonable explanation for the occurrence of some of these, and expect that the students will not repeat them. You may decide that some just aren't all that important. Some of those of lesser importance include chewing gum; putting their feet on another student's desk or a piece of classroom furniture; throwing spitballs; passing notes; leaving trash on the floor; and sleeping during your lecture. This last one is less than a major offense because you must take a great deal of responsibility in keeping your lectures interesting. If a student sleeps through one, it may be that you slipped up, or it may be that the student had a late night or just began taking some sort of legal narcotic or other medication that makes him or her sleepy. You will find out which because you are concerned about their welfare and will check with counselors, other teachers, and ask the student.

THE PROBLEM I have a girl who sleeps a lot in my classes and yet gets a B+ grade. I am hesitant to say anything to her because of that.

THE SOLUTION B+ is certainly respectable, but she may have a sleep disorder or some other physical problem. Talk to her and her parents.

Student Conduct Expectations

You must take the current climate of school and your classroom activities into consideration when thinking about student conduct. Let's look at some examples:

Get Shy Students Involved

The school wants to build community through student body participation in sports activities. Not all students have the ability to play sports and so some schools hold a pep rally on Friday afternoons, thereby shortening classes and allowing everyone to go outside for the rally if weather permits in order to build a stronger community. Most of the kids really get a kick out of the rally because it's a chance to scream and participate in some fun activities. Some students will want no part of this for various reasons, but usually it's because they are shy and are uncomfortable around large groups of people.

So, you have two different problems. What conduct is appropriate for those who participate and what is appropriate for those who don't? The first one is actually the easier one. Pep rallies mean screaming and cheering and laughing at the antics of the students who perform stunts so, no matter how much noise this creates it is acceptable. Safety becomes a major concern with this.

The kids who don't want anything to do with the activity may try to hang back inside the classroom or go to their locker, or to the restroom to be alone. It will be your job to find them, talk gently to them in an understanding tone to draw them out of their shell and get them to, at least, come to the rally site. I have done this many times, finding the shy ones in all the places mentioned and slowly, gently, yet firmly coaxing them to join everyone else. Their feeling of loneliness won't immediately disappear when they come into the presence of the other cheering, screaming students, but you will notice the evidence of fear in their face dissolve into one of having made a pleasant discovery. I only had to do this once with each child and, after that, they came to the rallies, although they continued to hang to the back of the crowd so others wouldn't notice them.

Some of you may think me harsh or uncaring, almost forcing the kids into awkward situations. Shy kids are better off left to themselves rather than embarrassing them by exposing them to a crowd of other kids. They stayed in the back, generally unseen and unnoticed by the others, yet the relieved expressions on their faces indicated that they began to feel more a part of our community by their proximity. We humans are social creatures. We need each other.

Let the Kids Make the Rules

Everything remains copacetic, with no changes from the prior school year. Believe it or not, this situation is a rarity.

Schools evolve, just like the rest of society, and this means change. But, assuming no change, the student conduct should reflect excellent adherence to all school rules and to your classroom rules once you have made them clear at the beginning of the year. Just give them a few weeks to learn your rules, since they will be somewhat different from those of the teachers they had the year before. After that time, clearly and firmly apply yours. Remember, kids actually want rules.

Here's a thought to consider. Let the students in on your rule making. Not only do students respond well to rules as long as they know and understand them, but they will even respond better if you empower them by getting their input in the setting of the rules. Dare you do this? Think about our democratic society versus a totalitarian regime. Do most of us feel better off making our own laws or having them foisted upon us by a dictator who knows (in his or her mind at least) what is best for us?

Field Trip Fun

Try this one. You want to take a field trip to the local historical museum. You know the many things that the students can learn from this visit, so you tell them about the trip and your ideas of what you expect them to learn. Okay, you exercised your assertiveness, now see if you can approach it this way.

Announce the field trip. Obviously you want to take the trip to expand on the current classroom lessons. Instead of following your announcement with telling them of your learning expectations, begin a meeting in which you ask for input on what they think they will see and what they might learn from that. Better yet, allow time for them to do some research, and then call a meeting. Ask them to designate a leader for the meeting to keep order and keep them on task. Another student should take notes on the ideas, unless the class is too young to write, in which case you do this. You only function as the adviser, stepping in only if the desig-nated leader loses control. By doing this they buy into the trip and should show eagerness not just to get out of school for a while, but to discover the answers to their questions.

Circle-up the Seats

When conducting a meeting, remember that the best way to seat the students for conversation that potentially involves everyone is a circle. Think of *King Arthur and the Knights of the Round Table*, where everyone appeared equal and could see each other for that all-important eye contact when speaking. If the students can gather their desks into a circle, that will work. Or they can sit on the floor in a circle. In either case, you just become part of a circle. Make sure they have enough background readings accomplished before this to make the discussion productive. You will just be amazed at what they come up with. This is a good exercise in problem solving and critical thinking. You will need more than two class periods to work this out, so prepare ahead of time for that. When they have finished the meeting and have their goals in mind, ask them where they did their research.

Your students now have learned the proper behavior and responsibilities for different classroom and out-of-classroom activities. Your next step in this rule setting process involves getting the parents' support for the result. Send them a report of the proceedings and the results. Ask for their comments.

THE PROBLEM My students are always complaining that I take the fun out of activities. I don't know how I am supposed to keep things entertaining while making sure everyone behaves.

THE SOLUTION Explain to your students how important they are in every activity, whether it be a pep rally, field trip, or class discussion. When they understand that their behavior and participation matters, they will begin to understand why the rules matter and how much fun things can be when everyone behaves.

There Will Be an Open House. What Are You to Do?

First, an open house is not a time for parent-teacher conferences. The principal's overall objective will be to assure the parents that their children will get the best possible education that the facility and faculty have to offer.

You can expect a presentation of teachers as a group, and then they will be introduced individually to the parents or guardians and any new students and their younger siblings who came along with them. You should make it a fun and informative occasion. At an open house it is your job to inform the guests about your subjects and tout the excellence of the faculty's educational expertise, as well as the entire staff's concern for the students entrusted to you.

One approach to handling this is to have a mini school day, with the bell ringing for the change of classes every five or ten minutes. The guests walk around from room to room based on their child's class schedule. Some senior students usually get involved in directing the guests so they don't get lost. You stay in your classroom to greet the guests with a warm handshake and a smile as you state your name. Make sure you have placed something outside your door indicating the classes held in your room, and your name. Also print your name on the board or have an interactive electronic whiteboard or other multimedia presentation to show the visitors, allowing several minutes for questions.

Alternatively, the principal will ask the faculty to sit at assigned places in the library or gym so the guests may line up to speak to their children's teachers. This format won't allow for a multimedia presentation, so plan to spend the few minutes you have with each guest introducing yourself and providing a synopsis of your classes. Make careful observations of distinguishing features of the guests to build your memory base.

Politeness is essential during an open house, as it is any time that you represent the school. Do not forget your manners. Stand and shake each visitor's hand, and invite them to sit down. You may have time to give a brief report on their child's progress, so make sure you have that information available. Also, don't forget to dress up for this occasion. Wear your opening-day clothes.

Use the open house as a good tool for developing rapport with the parents or guardians, thereby building their confidence in you and support for what you can accomplish with their children. The next chapter will discuss the many ways to build those critical bonds with your students. The open house should reinforce those efforts by gaining the backing, encouragement, and assistance of the parents and guardians.

THE PROBLEM During the last open house a parent cornered me and I couldn't make a presentation to any others. I saw them start to enter my room and, upon seeing me in serious conversation with someone else, they left.

THE SOLUTION Stand back a bit from the doorway of your classroom, greet the guests, and gradually move toward the center of the room. Most parents will take that as a signal to sit in a student desk. If one doesn't sit, politely ask him or her to do so, offering a seat. Make your presentation and make sure it lasts until the bell rings for a rotation of guests. This is your opportunity to thank them again for coming and usher them toward the door. If a guest wants to stay, gently remind him or her that more people are coming. If he or she wants to discuss more, you can make an appointment for another time.

Are your appearance, your attitude, and your rules important? Yes, so let's sum up:

1. Dressing for success means to dress as a professional, not as a student. You don't want to be confused for a student by the students.

2. Maintain a positive mental attitude, and be responsible for your actions.
3. Respect the students as persons. They will return that respect.
4. Do not ever appear pompous or you will lose your audience—the students.
5. Don't be afraid to set your own classroom rules. Just make sure you know and follow the school rules first.
6. Look upon the annual open house as an opportunity for building rapport with parents and guardians.

CHAPTER 8

Winning Them Over—The Teacher Who Bonds, Wins

The importance of bonding with your students cannot be emphasized enough. You will have students with varying capabilities. Make it an important part of your mission to build on this bond. Dr. Norman Vincent Peale in his book *The Tough-Minded Optimist* tells a story of how, when traveling to a speaking engagement, he decided to lunch with a local Rotary Club. A Rotarian himself, he had always tried to attend at least one meeting a month in spite of his heavy travel requirements as a motivational speaker.

This particular day he entered the hotel room where the local Rotarians were preparing to hold their luncheon meeting. He found an empty chair at the table, sat down, and proceeded to introduce himself to those around him. A fellow Rotarian sitting next to him said that he had completely run out of enthusiasm and he knew Dr. Peale always tried to sell enthusiasm. He said he had read all of Dr. Peale's books, and thought they really made sense, but they just didn't click for him, and he wanted to know what to do.

Dr. Peale watched the man's body language as he spoke. His slumped shoulders, frowning face and brooding eyes emphasized the sadness ripping away at his heart. Dr. Peale knew the man didn't just want conversation. He needed an answer. The answer that Dr. Peale gave doesn't matter; what matters is that the man respected Dr. Peale not only because of his public speaking abilities, but for his insight into the depth of a real person and the expectation that Dr. Peale would help him in his crisis.

You're On—an Introduction

That inevitable opening day has arrived. You have on your best dress or suit, and the bell rings. No more practicing for this day. Stand by the door and shake their hands to welcome them. Tell the students to sit wherever they would like. They like that. If you have decided to use a seating chart, you'll get around to that soon enough. In their minds at this moment, they are sizing you up. If both you and they have been at the school for a few years, they've already heard rumors about you. If you are new, they want to figure you out as soon as possible. Will you grade easy or tough? What kind of tests do you give? How strict are you?

Learning something in your class is way down their list of priorities that day. On that very day, they decide whether they like and respect you or that you're the biggest jerk in the world. God help you if they choose the latter. It is very tough overcoming that. If you don't want them to conclude that you are a jerk, you must do something about it.

You wonder if your apprehension or nervousness shows. You have written your name and the course on the board, so they know whether or not they have come to the right place. You have arranged the desks so that you can be close to them when lecturing.

You begin by standing silently in front of them for a few seconds before you speak—a "dramatic pause." Since they don't know what you intend to do next, they also become silent. Now you can speak.

Tell them your name again, and talk a bit about your background. Speak clearly and just loud enough for the people farthest away from you to hear. Begin your talk about the course and how it interconnects with other courses they are taking. Pause and ask them what other courses they are taking (you should already know this through your pre-first-day review). They will take that question as a sign of your interest in them. And it is a legitimate interest, because you are trying to use everything you can to get to know them.

Listen to their responses and explain further how your course interconnects with the others. Continue doing this throughout the year. Kids, and even teens, cannot understand how certain courses will help them in adult life or actually fit with the other courses they have to take. Now comes the hard part for you—remembering their names. If you teach high school, you may get more than one hundred new faces to connect to names every year. Some will already know your name, but *all* of them expect you to know theirs.

THE PROBLEM The First Day . . . I know first impressions are always the hardest to shake. I need to make a good one so my students will like and respect me.

THE SOLUTION Greet them like adults. Meet them at the door and shake their hands. Introduce yourself and your course, and explain its importance. Do so in a very straightforward and professional manner.

Naming Tools: Seating Chart Alternatives

Everyone knows how to use a seating chart. Right? In my first year I set up my chart upside down. For some reason I had everyone flip-flopped, and I hadn't yet discovered using V-shaped seating. The minute class started, confusion reigned. I called boys by girls' names and vice versa for about the first six or seven tries. The kids politely corrected me. I thanked them, went to my podium, took out my chart, wadded it up, and threw it in the wastebasket. I looked at them and said, "Well, I guess that didn't work." I laughed at my mistake and so did they. It was the first of many laughs we had together. I didn't realize it but, by showing them I could make a mistake and laugh it off, they felt more at ease with me. We had begun bonding.

Seating Charts

Obviously, if you use seating charts, get them right. Seating charts really do help you learn the students' names quickly without them having to repeatedly tell you, and they like that.

One way to build respect with high schoolers, especially the juniors and seniors, is to let them choose their seats. It's very possible they haven't had a teacher who allowed them to do that before, and it makes them feel older and more respected. It may sound like a small thing but, like running that marathon, you have to take the first step. Respect and trust are feelings that take time to mature. Having said that, how, then, do you figure out who is who? And how do you control friends and boyfriend/girlfriend situations when they are permitted to sit next to each other? If you have permitted the students to sit wherever they choose on that first day, say something like this: "You are juniors (or seniors) and as such, the upper classmen. You are the ones the younger kids look up to and follow. That should feel pretty cool. Enjoy that feeling. You earned it. Don't forget, with every privilege comes a responsibility. In this case the responsibility is to set that good example of being a student who wants to learn. You also have assumed the responsibility to help me learn not only your names, but who you really are. I would like for you to identify yourself by at least your first name when called upon, and I will repeat it. When I return assignments that will help me. And, if you will always sit in the seats you have chosen today, in a very short time I will know all of you and I will call you by name so you don't have to keep giving me reminders. Is that okay?" They always nod in the affirmative. So you continue, "Good, I will do my best to get your names right as fast as possible."

I have yet to have anyone object to that approach, and they easily volunteer their names every chance they get until I know them because I have empowered them with that gesture, albeit small, of trust and responsibility by accepting their choice of seating. I usually have all their names memorized by the second class because I call on them a lot that first day. I use repetition with some time in between to allow the brain to make associations, and yet it's frequent enough that I generally have seen and heard from each one three times. Remember, though, that this approach doesn't work very well with the younger kids. They just don't have the maturity to get it.

THE PROBLEM Regarding seating charts—I let my students decide where they are going to sit, but they always end up talking and disrupting class because they sit near their friends.

THE SOLUTION Make them understand that choosing their seats comes with responsibility. They need to act maturely in order for them to be treated maturely.

Yearbook Pictures

Here's a way to use the yearbook as the primary name-learning tool. Just before the opening day browse through the yearbook, if the school has one. Then on the first day of regular classes, after the opening day's introductions, you can continue building on your name recognition file. At the beginning of every class on the first day, read the attendance chart aloud. By watching each student respond, you continue building the match between the person and the name. Then, at the end of the day, take out the yearbook and look at their faces and names again. Do this just one time, but focus on the task. Then go home. Sleep on it. Your subconscious mind will begin making the associations.

THE PROBLEM I am having a very difficult time remembering all my students' names.

THE SOLUTION First, watch each student respond as you call roll. Then after class get a yearbook and go through it looking up the kids on your roster. And finally, sleep on it.

Abraham Lincoln Method

If you have no yearbook to access, you need to use another approach. Try the Abe Lincoln method again, as described in Chapter 5: read and mull, read and mull. On the first day of classes, take attendance by walking up to the students as they acknowledge their names, and repeat them. Look carefully into each student's eyes and face, say the name, and ask if you said it correctly. If you did, look back at your attendance sheet and look at the name and check it off. If you did not say it correctly, repeat the name after the student says it. Be sure to *really* look at the name. Don't just glance at it. Remember, the students *really* expect you to know them, so concentrate on this. It's very important.

THE PROBLEM I teach elementary school students and don't have a yearbook I can use. What am I supposed to do? There are so many names.

THE SOLUTION Act like Abe. Read and mull, read and mull. Call their name during roll. Look into their face. Say their name again. Ask for correction and then look back at their name on the attendance.

Getting-to-Know-You Exercises

You are the most important thing your students want to know at the beginning of their school year. How you will test them? How you will grade them? How many big assignments will you give them? Don't let these questions distract you for very long.

Yes, they do want to know these things, but in all likelihood, unless they are attending your school for the first time, they already have gotten those answers from the students who took your course last year. The only other kids who wouldn't already have the answers are the lower elementary, those in grades one through three. They have yet to catch on to, or become a part of, the gossip system.

Answer the students' questions and begin to tell them anecdotes that provide answers to their bigger questions. When the question comes up about how much homework you give and how you grade it, the easy answer would be that you give homework every time you cover a new topic and that you expect it completed and turned in on time. You could add that you grade it on a scale starting at 100 percent, for getting all the answers in the homework assignment correct, down to zero for not turning it in. Or another option is that you look over the assignments and, if a student completed the assignment as requested, you give it a check mark. Then at the end of each quarter you add up the check marks (value 100 percent each) and then average them to arrive at an overall grade for homework. For example, there were fifteen required assignments. A student did thirteen resulting in acquiring thirteen check marks. Thirteen times 100 percent equals 1,300 percent. Divide 1,300 percent by 15 and the resulting grade is 86.8 percent, or a B.

Alternatively, if you wish to calculate their homework grade on the percentage of problems or questions they answered correctly, you can have them grade each other's papers the next class. In the case of math problems, they calculate the grade based on 100 percent for showing the formula, the procedure used, and the correct answer. If the formula is missing, they deduct 20 percent. If the formula is there but the calculation is missing, even if they have the correct answer, they deduct 20 percent. If the formula and the calculation are missing, even though they have the correct answer, they deduct 40 percent. You record the grades each day. Add them and divide by the number of required assignments for the period of time involved and post the grades so they know how they are doing. Or you may have your own specific method. All of this is good information, but not the answer to the real question.

The real question was quite different. What the kids really asked was, "I heard from kids who had your class last year that you give a lot of homework. Why do you assign so much?" How do you answer that, since it was implied and not actually asked? If, for example, you are teaching an English class, tell the students that during the course of the year they will read many different types of literature. Some of it will be hard to understand. When you know you are reading a poem that introduces a lot of new poetic techniques, making it difficult to understand, you will go over those techniques in class. You will work on some examples and maybe even have the students write something on their own in order to practice.

Or, if you teach a science class there will be lots of new terminology for them to learn. Design homework assignments to learn new terms and reinforce the scientific basis. If you teach elementary school, every subject you teach will have an element of the need to remember information and build on it, and one of the best ways to succeed in this is practicing on their own.

In all those cases you will give a homework assignment that reinforces what was covered in class. Going back to the example of an English class, you would tell the students that you will expect them to use proper grammar and complete sentences in their homework assignments, so there will not be any yes-or-no questions relating to the reading.

No matter which subject you teach, tell the students that you will keep a chart of completed homework. Each time an assignment is completed as required, they will get either a check mark or a specific grade as previously discussed.

Now, having said all that, follow up by telling them that you know that no two people think exactly alike. That means no two people write exactly the same, and the differences between their methods of writing reflect their voices. It's the students' voices you want to hear when you read their homework assignments, whether the assignment requires answering questions that followed a particular reading or an in-depth writing assignment such as a literary book analysis. And, whether dealing with math, science or a language, or any other subject, they will have to express their thoughts on paper and so this same idea applies.

This is an awfully complex answer to the seemingly simple question, "How much homework do you give?" But that's part of reading between the lines in order to let the students get to know you, and you them. You want them to get to know you as soon as possible. And getting to know you means under-standing how you think, which lets them better anticipate how you will test them and what questions you will ask—and, therefore, what they need to learn.

If they are home doing their homework and get stuck, they may call a friend. If, between the two of them, they still don't get it they will give up, believing it is too far above their heads. But, if they feel you are approachable, they will discuss it with you when they return to school. Without that feeling of approachability, there is a strong chance they will stop doing homework. This is detrimental to their learning, and begins a slippery slope toward dropping out of school.

THE PROBLEM My kids choose to quit doing their homework and turn in nothing instead of coming to me before or after class to ask questions.

THE SOLUTION Let them know who you are and what you expect from day one. If they view you as approachable, they are going to approach you. Make them feel like you understand where they are coming from, and they will ask you for help.

Getting-to-Trust-You Exercises

You have discussed the course, grading, homework, and your approach to these. You told them a bit about how you came to teaching at that school, and some of your teaching or other background. Now here's a tough one for you to express, but you should do it nonetheless. Tell them you love them and there's no place you would rather be than here with them. If you don't really feel that way, you should seriously consider another profession. Kids decide almost instantly how they feel about someone, and they want you to love them. No matter their age, all children want their parents and teachers to love them.

Follow that by explaining you have read their portfolios, you have had some discussions with other teachers, and you love teaching kids like them. Later in the year, maybe after semester break, make sure to remind them of this. They can never hear it too often. By the midpoint of the year they will have gotten to know you and trust you, and saying this again will make the bond stronger. If you love them, it follows that you trust them. You must trust them if you expect them to trust you.

Someone once said, "Words are cheap; show me." That all-important trust between you and your students will build through consistency. You tell them that you will give them a test on a specific date on a certain topic, and you deliver it on that date. You describe your grading system, and they see it in action. If a student comes to you with a reason why he or she will hand in an assignment late, and you tell him or her that it's okay and you won't deduct points, don't change that when it comes in and you grade it. You must always do things the same way unless you give prior notice. Remember, consistency equals trust.

As you already know, I normally have my students' desks arranged in a V pattern. There was a time when I planned to show a movie once we reached a certain point in our studies, but I forgot to tell the students that I would show a movie during the next class. In order for all of them to have a good close view, I moved all the desks toward the front, about four rows deep, and very close together. When they came in the room, they nearly freaked! A couple of the boys even started moving the desks to their normal positions before I could explain.

Another time I had decided we needed to have an open discussion of some of our latest readings, and so without prior notice, I moved the desks into a couple of circles to facilitate discussion. Again the students freaked out and started moving desks before I could explain. I quickly told them they were to hold a discussion of the differences and similarities among the elements of literary technique used in the three pieces they'd read. I gave them thirty minutes for the discussion, and told them to create a list of the differences and similarities that they all agreed on, and to select someone to write the list on the interactive electronic whiteboard. From there we got into discussions about why they had made the selections. What a class! We were still at it when the bell rang at the end of the eighty-minute class.

In both instances the students enjoyed what we did so much, they forgot about the surprise of seeing the desks rearranged. Nevertheless, I will not forget again to give them advance notice and to let them move the desks wherever they want. Remember that no one likes change, especially kids, even though they would tell you just the opposite. The overriding message here is consistency.

I remember once telling one of my managers, who had continual employee problems and high turnover, that he could perform like a nice guy all the time or he could act like a jerk all the time. People can live with consistency even if they don't like it. I also told him he couldn't continue acting nice one day and like a jerk the next. That causes confusion and insecurity, and the result will not be pleasant. This is the same method I apply to my classroom.

THE PROBLEM My students are always confused and don't listen to me. I try to change up my teaching style and attitude daily so that they will not get bored.

THE SOLUTION Stay consistent. You will lose your kids if you do not remain consistent. Consistency is the key to trust, and trust is the key to successful classroom management.

Open Door Policy: When and Why You're Available to Them

You must make yourselves available for student and parent conferences. This supports the bonding and communication needed for a successful learning experience for the student, and teaching experience for you. You will experience a conundrum, however, involving where to find the time to be available while also preparing for classes, grading papers and tests, attending faculty meetings, becoming involved as an adviser or mentor, and still having a personal life. Let's analyze this.

You teach in your classroom a minimum of five and a half hours a day. Administration will normally expect you to arrive thirty minutes before the first class and stay another thirty after the last class. That comes to approximately six and a half hours a day, so what's the problem? Oh wait, you must check homework and grade papers, and research teaching materials. And guaranteed, the thirty minutes you have in the morning before the students arrive will be filled with picking up memos, mail, and attendance sheets from your box, opening your room, straightening desks, writing assignments on the board, and testing your computer and other electronic equipment to make sure everything works. You will also read the mail, sort graded papers for distribution, and write reminders to yourself to give some students information, take books or other items

left in your room to the office, and on, and on, and on. You should realize that you need an hour rather than the minimum half hour in the mornings, so plan for that. Then there's that open door.

Always, and I mean always, unless holding a private meeting, have your door open. You want the students to know they can walk in anytime. The same goes for your planning period but, since that occurs during the class day, you will get very few, if any, walk-ins, so use that time wisely.

Announce to your students that the best time to meet with you is immediately after the last class or, if they want to set a specific time, make it before class begins. I hold most of my parent conferences either with or without their child, in the morning before the first bell. Again, the meeting can't go on too long because the bell will call it to a halt. Having that potential tends to make the parents arrive on time and allows us to get right to the point of the meeting. This may sound a little cold, but if you prepared well and welcome them with your best smile and handshake, the need for small talk withers away quickly. The parents will respect that you want to get down to business because many times they have a complaint and it's difficult for them to express it if left to their own timing. You have created a win-win situation. They get over any reluctance and you get to the point in order to work on a solution, all within your timing.

THE PROBLEM I want my kids to stop in whenever they have a problem, but with all my teaching duties I never feel like I have any time.

THE SOLUTION Be smart and schedule your time. Give yourself an hour before school to do daily tasks as well as meet with parents. Leave your door open whenever you are in the classroom, and let your students know when you are available.

What They'll Learn—and Why It Matters

Back in the dark ages when I went to school, my parents told me that whatever the teacher taught, I should not question. By and large, learning was a memorization process. Looking back on that method of teaching, I wonder where I picked up critical thinking skills (my wife wonders if I actually have any, but that's for another discussion). I do not want my students learning in the dark ages; I want them to be able to compete.

One of the greatest challenges in the world of business is competition. Won't our students need the ability to figure out how to make a product better than the competition's, or get their product to market faster, or provide better service than the others? Or just plain make smarter decisions than the competition? Of course they will. You must explain to them why organic chemistry, or algebraic formulas, or knowledge of history is so important. They will definitely need to speak at least one foreign language—right now the emphasis is on Spanish, but Eastern languages, such as Chinese, are becoming more and more important. And if your students don't at least have a basic understanding of computers, they may find themselves on the outside looking in. On top of all this, if they can't get their ideas across in the form of clear, meaningful, written communication, they will be in serious trouble. Don't forget this.

Keep abreast of world events, read voraciously, and travel when you can. Doing these things will give you the background to explain why what you teach matters to them.

I had the opportunity to live in France and travel all over Europe and parts of Scandinavia during my business career. I had taken three years of Latin and one of Spanish in high school, so when I had to take a crash course in French I was able to succeed with it. After only three months of living in France I could speak French fluently. I don't think I could have caught on so quickly if I hadn't taken Latin.

I remember one day having lunch in Groningen, Netherlands, with two Dutch businessmen and two who were Flemish. They each spoke five languages, and switched from one to the other for practice. At least they said that's what they were doing. You see my disadvantage. Most Americans can't imagine speaking that many languages. Well, the world continues to get smaller and smaller, and you must do what you can to get your students to understand that.

It all comes down to critical thinking, really. If your students know why you teach something, they are better equipped to build on that knowledge. The greatest thrill of teaching occurs when students graduate, move on with their lives, and return one day to tell you that, because of the way you challenged them to learn, they are successful in a career and happy with themselves.

THE PROBLEM The world is a lot different than when I was in school. I am trying to make sure my students will be able to compete once they graduate.

THE SOLUTION Make them understand the importance of education and they will want to be educated. Let them question you and your teaching. They will learn better and more if they understand why they are being taught.

What They'll Like—and Why It Matters

You have to know going into this profession that you will have students who really hate school. They hate the courses they have to take, they hate some of their teachers, and they just plain hate having to be there. Veteran teachers have had to deal with plenty of this type of kids. The biggest issue with them—discipline—is discussed in Chapter 11. The rest of the students will like some classes and dislike others. Your job is to make your class as interesting as possible so your students will find learning interesting and, ideally, fun. You and they both will be winners if they enjoy the learning process, even if they don't get the best grades in your class. After all, if your students graduate from high school with the desire to learn new things and to understand others, they will become successful, productive citizens. If they choose to go on to obtain higher-level learning and further expand their minds because you made their history, math, science, or English course interesting, pat yourself on the back!

If you can relate what you teach in the classroom to what goes on in the students' extracurricular world, they will enjoy it. Most sports and games use a lot of math and science. Chess, Sudoku, card games, many video games, and even NASCAR racing require critical thinking skills that students can develop in language arts as well as science or computer classes.

Do you know at what speed a car will become airborne when making a forty-degree turn? Should the knight be moved to e3 position and sacrificed to move your rook to f7? How many ways do you have to go through a seemingly impenetrable wall to get to the next level of the video game? How hard, and at what trajectory, do you have to kick a soccer ball to get it into the goal from fifty feet in front? Do you see where this is going? These are questions that your class will want to figure out, and they will enjoy meeting the challenge.

THE PROBLEM Some of my students zone out during my lectures. How can I get my students interested in the material I have to cover?

THE SOLUTION Relate it to something they enjoy. If your students see how they can apply what they are learning in the classroom to something they enjoy outside, they will be interested. And interested students are good students.

What They'll Find Challenging—and Why It Shouldn't Matter

This goes back to that reason for your students being in school in the first place. If never challenged, a mind, like an unused muscle, atrophies and becomes useless. Creativity and critical thinking present the biggest challenges to kids today. Many studies show that watching too much television and too many movies stifles creativity. Why? Because the viewer doesn't have to imagine what the character or the scene looks like. It takes imagination to create anything. It takes critical thinking and imagination to find out why something doesn't perform the way you want it to, and then to fix and improve on it. Creativity doesn't just apply to art and writing. We need to have creative people to handle all the challenges of a dynamic society.

Challenge your students, and feel no guilt when they groan and moan. One of the activities I do in teaching creative writing starts with placing a series of pictures on the front board. I ask my students to study the pictures and then, when a picture speaks to them, to sit down and start writing until I say stop. This blows most of the kids' minds because I don't give them any parameters. Another exercise I use is to give them a phrase and tell them to finish it and then write a complete paragraph using it. Sometimes I stack a few things from my desk on a student's desk in the front of the room before class begins. After the bell rings and they are all settled down, I put the items behind my desk where they can't see them. I ask them to list and describe the items they saw on the desk, and write a short story using all of them. This tests their observation skills as well as their ability to make a story out of mundane things they see every day. They really struggle with this one, but some do such a phenomenal job I get tears of joy when I read their work.

You must understand why you have to continually challenge your students. Every class should be different, and therein lies your own challenge. If you work at it you will reap unbelievable rewards as you see these kids do things they never thought possible.

Although teaching isn't meant to be a popularity contest, <u>win them over</u>, and you're halfway to teaching them something.

Let's summarize this chapter:

1. Find your best way to learn your students' names as soon as possible. They know you, and expect you to know them. If you expect to develop a bond of trust and respect where learning may take place, you need to do this.
2. There are many ways to let them know the real you. The best way is to tell them, and then prove it through daily practices.
3. Develop trust through consistency.
4. Make yourself accessible. Be available as often as possible.
5. It matters what they learn, and they'll learn better when you show them that you know what they like. That is a major component to understanding.
6. Challenge them even though they object. The real world certainly will.

CHAPTER 9

Debriefing

Taking Stock

Ever ask yourself "What was I thinking?" Or, "How did that happen? That wasn't what I wanted to do." I hope so, because that means you pay attention to results.

Your Performance: Just What Did You Expect?

Any good manager knows that you will have no idea of success or failure unless you have something by which to measure or compare your actual results. You must have standards. To use a golfing cliché, standards tell you what the par is for the course. You must set standards for yourself early on. You first-year teachers may say at this point, "That's easy for you to say; you have a teaching track record. With what do I measure?"

We've discussed the concepts of respect, bonding, dressing for success, understanding everything about the school where you teach and its rules, and most important, planning. All of these have the student at their center. We have focused almost our entire attention toward the student, but you have yourself and your career to consider so you need a way to stop and look at it as dispassionately as possible to evaluate success or failure. Let's take a look at standards you can use to measure your performance.

1. Discuss issues with your mentor. Topics should range from specific disciplinary problems to your selection of grading methods, your lecturing time in class, your dress, and on and on.
2. Get an excellent administrative review report.
3. Comply fully with any recommendations made by a peer review.
4. Establish a start time and a finish time for normal days.
5. Spend no more than two hours each evening grading papers, and no more than eight hours during the course of the weekend, for a total of eighteen hours each week.
6. Create tests that properly evaluate student learning.
7. Create and keep good parental relations with a minimum of complaints. Set your minimum at some arbitrary figure based on a percentage of the number of students you teach or will teach. Ask other teachers what they think their percentages for these are.
8. Establish and practice good communication techniques to keep both students and parents informed of course curriculum and student performance relative thereto.
9. Create and maintain good relations with office and maintenance personnel.
10. Become involved in student activities (during the first year, one adviser role), slowly expanding enough to enhance student bonding without jeopardizing having a personal life.
11. Establish and maintain good relationships with other teaching staff members, and share student knowledge where possible.
12. Help students prepare so that their performance on standardized tests is equal to or better than the previous year.
13. Assist students with recommendation letters to colleges, resulting in acceptance.

Okay, this list makes teaching look complicated. How will you ever do all of these things, let alone keep track of your performance? Simple. Post this list in a place where you can't help but see it every day. None of these are quantifiable, say the math teachers. How can you possibly grade yourself on these? Admittedly, if you are just out of college or have come into teaching from another profession, you will encounter difficulty in doing this, especially if you don't start the year with a list already compiled. Set yours up right now. I'll wait.

Now, let's get into more detail about judging your performance based on the standards in the previous list.

THE PROBLEM A student who really isn't college material, and doesn't apply himself very well with the talents he does have, asked me to write a college recommendation letter.

THE SOLUTION The guidance counselor can help in this instance. You don't want to confront the student alone because two things can happen. One is that the student becomes deflated and drops any idea of higher education. The other is that the parents sue you. There's an old adage that success in college is 95 percent desire and 5 percent intelligence. You want to let them know that college isn't for everybody, and there are many successful businesses that were started by people without college degrees, and that those who want to go to college, really need to want to go to college.

---

1. If your school has a mentoring program for first-year teachers, it will also have a mentor binder in which you and your mentor will keep notes of discussions. This binder should have a list of things for the mentor to discuss with you. Make sure you get a copy. If these binders don't exist, make your own notes after any meeting with your mentor. Your goal in doing this is to be able to look back periodically and see what issues have come up, as well as your mentor's suggested solutions.

If you have taught for a long time, you may have become stale, frustrated, or bored. Keep a log of situations and how you handled them. You can then review this log periodically to look for ways to improve grading techniques, or testing that doesn't seem to work. Perhaps in reviewing the test results it appears obvious that students managed to find out the questions that would be on the test, and maybe even the answers. You can change the test questions once you see a pattern. On the other hand, your students may not have been performing well on standardized tests. With this tool you can compare your teaching information with what the standard tests require. You may not want to direct your teaching to standardized testing, but you certainly can make improvements in what or how you teach by attending seminars developed for this purpose. You may reap a side benefit of renewed enthusiasm from attending these types of seminars.

2. Although what you learn from your administrative review depends on the viewpoint of your principal, you will always learn something. Ask for a copy of the report after discussion. Take notes at your evaluation meeting in case you can't get the actual report. When you look at this, keep in mind that the principal's point of view will be slanted in favor of the school's mission and goals because those are the measurements that the board will use when evaluating the principal. That's good, because as you focus all your energies on the daily teaching experience of lecturing, testing, grading, and so on, your view of the bigger picture can easily become foggy. Bring it back into focus and make sure you add to it.

3. Your peer review looks more at the details of how you conduct your class than does the principal or administrator review. Your fellow teachers normally will give little thought to the big picture and more to the comments you make and questions you ask in class. Hopefully, you get to pick the teacher to do this review. If so, don't focus on friend-ship, but on skills and course taught by that teacher. You want a teacher who knows your subject to really get a good, helpful review. Get a copy of the notes, the same as for an adminis-trative review. Review the notes from the peer review imme-diately, because if the observer saw the need for change in something over which you have control, it affects the students and needs immediate attention.

4. Start early and finish late. If that was your goal, so be it, but it is not a specific enough goal. In other words, what does early or late mean? Say, for example, you start normal teaching days an hour before class starts, and stay one hour after the last class. Did you do this like clockwork? I would guess not, but how would you know you had done something not par for your course, if you don't know what par is? What's the purpose of being so punctual? It gives you structure, and assists in evening meal times, as well as getting-up times. So, you look back and find that you have stayed late by as much as an hour to two hours twice a week. Look at the reasons for this. If you stayed late for parent-teacher conferences that you set up, maybe you could have held those in the mornings and also shortened the time involved. Then you could have gotten home earlier to do more grading. In any event, you now know about them and have the ability to change that behavior if you choose.

5. You really blew this one. You worked until nine and ten in the evening twenty times, and spent fifteen hours grading papers on each of five weekends. Take a look at your actual testing and grading method as well as the way you grade homework papers. Perhaps you could achieve the same learning experience for your students if you gave tests for which you could use Scantron grading sheets rather than comprehensive writing. Maybe you spend way too much time reading homework. Perhaps you could change from read-ing entire essays to skimming titles and only looking at the grammar used on the first page, leaving it to the students to follow through on your corrections by rewriting and making changes throughout the papers, and then resubmitting them to you. Now that's more like the real world.

6. Did your tests compare favorably with the results of standardized testing? In other words, have you taught the material according to the state's standards and the syllabus and course curriculum? If not, look for variances. Where are they? Isolate these and change the questions and also the teaching of related material.

7. If you are new to teaching, check with experienced teachers to determine the type and number of parental complaints. Be sure to ask if they systematically contact parents, and if so, how. If you are experienced, you may still need to check with your peers if you've never done this. In either case the research will allow you to establish a base line of parental complaints. If this is your first time to do this, set your goal for the first grading period at the same level as the other teachers you contacted. Then each quarter lower the goal and improve your parental contacts.

8. Your original plan called for using the school's Web site to post lectures on major units along with quarter and semester final lectures, book analysis requirements, essay requirements, and homework assignments, thus providing both students and parents with exactly what you cover in your class.

Send e-mails to parents when students fail to do assignments or make up tests they missed. Also send e-mails to parents when students perform particularly well.

9. Get to know where all the supplies are so you can get them without disturbing the office workers. Also make it a point to greet the maintenance and luncheon personnel.

10. Get involved in one student activity as an adviser or mentor for a student. Take a look at clubs, service organizations, and sports teams, both intramural and interscholastic, and determine whether you want to somehow become involved. Make a notation of the club or clubs you want to work with in future years.

11. **Spend at least three lunch periods a week in the teacher's lounge to discuss things with other faculty members,** and maybe even find a new friend. Listen to and become involved in teacher conversations whenever possible.

12. **Get standardized test scores of your students and see how they stack up with the other department results from your school.**

13. Make sure your door is open to any senior who wants to discuss your writing a letter of recommendation for college entrance. **Keep track of letters.**

Their Performance: Were Your Expectations Too High or Low?

Does the infamous statistical bell curve apply here? As you undoubtedly already know, a bell curve is a graph representing the standard normal deviation in grades. In the case of measuring the results of classes, you would use the x axis to represent the grade of A, B, C, D, or F, and the y axis to represent the number of students receiving the grades.

For example, assume you have a class of thirty. Three received an A, five received a B, fifteen received a C, five received a D, and two received an F. If you were to plot these numbers on a graph, you would get a nearly perfect bell-shaped curve. So what does that mean? It simply tells you that the grades distributed in a normal fashion resulting in a normal spread of results, which means you have done your job well. No one really expects all of your students to get A's, or D's. The result obtained in the example here would seem to indicate you had done your job of teaching your students, and that they are a normal group.

That's the perfect world, of course. Within the group of grades you should take a look at the individual grades, keeping an eye out for differences from previous grades, quarter to quarter. The most alarming, and therefore, the most in need of attention, is a student with a huge drop in grades. Discuss this with the student, the guidance counselor, and the parents. This change could mean drug use, changes in outside relationships, or many other things that the parents and counselors would need to handle.

Identifying Potential Problems

This area has become one of the most difficult and potentially explosive of any you will encounter. You may discover things you really don't like about your teaching skills or ability to stay cool under pressure. You must, however, manage yourself the same way you manage your classes.

Keep a Journal—More than Just a Log

You already have your daily planner or a calendar of some fashion. Now you need to think about your personal feelings. After all, even if everything you do works for the students, it still may not work for you. Keep a record of your feelings in a file in your recorder. You can dictate it on your way home at the end of the day.

Make comments such as, "I put them in groups today to create poetry using the techniques we have learned up to now and they all seemed to respond well by working hard at it. Yet, I saw several groups of the boys who still focus on writing about their sport. I keep telling myself that's okay, but I really want them to expand their horizons. Maybe I expect too much in that regard."

Or, "I wonder if I don't pay enough attention to what goes on in the hallways. I want to focus on the subject matter of my courses, and really dislike the distractions that take place in this high school environment."

Notice that you don't have to work on solutions; just record your random thoughts.

THE PROBLEM Many of my days are so hectic because of dealing with the challenges of my students' learning abilities that all I want to do when I get in my car at night is go straight home and relax.

THE SOLUTION Not only do you need to relax; take a nap. Make sure it isn't too long or it will interfere with your sleep at night. Have your spouse wake you or set an alarm. You will wake feeling miserable, so sit up, keeping your eyes closed. Relax, letting the tension slip out of your body. Open your eyes. Put your hands over your head and stretch and yawn. Open your eyes and stand up slowly. In only a minute or two a new energy will come upon you and you will be ready to tackle the homework. The time taken by the short nap will be more than made up with the efficiency of a rested mind. That efficiency will allow you to accomplish more during your evening allotment of time so you can have more time during the day to deal with the other matters and not feel so harried.

Allow for Personal Space

Prioritize your daily activities to make sure you accomplish the most important things. As an example, assume that back at the beginning of the year you planned to introduce some new concepts during the second quarter because they fit best then. The second quarter looms near. You have set up your current quarter-ending tests and have everything graded, so you need to begin reviewing the material for the next quarter and planning for the introduction of the new concepts. Don't procrastinate. Do it.

It may seem too structured at first, but write down the times you get up in the morning, leave for work, spend planning, spend grading papers, etc. and analyze them closely in order to determine their relative importance. For example, if you are trying to grade papers as soon as the school day ends, and find your mind wandering, or sleepiness causing you to lose concentration, save making copies for that time so you can walk to the copy room. That may be enough physical activity to get past the sleepiness and you will also accomplish making the copies. Make sure you leave some personal time even if it's only a five- or ten-minute break every hour. Plan to do something over the weekend you've wanted to do for a long time. As your efficiency grows so will your personal time.

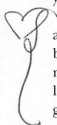

Love yourself, and what you do. Get up every morning and thank God for the opportunity to teach for another day, because you love it. Your head will be spinning at the end of many days your first year, so do things like yoga, or read a light novel just before bed, whatever relaxes you so you can get a good night's sleep.

THE PROBLEM I am a new teacher and so was very serious the first quarter. Then I tried loosening up during the second quarter and my students just didn't get my brand of teasing.

THE SOLUTION The differences in the dynamics of different classes are very interesting. Not all twelve-year-olds are the same. Not all seventeen-year-olds have reached the same level of maturity. A class will take on the personality of the de facto leader; in other words, the personality of the group within the class that has the highest level of maturity. Kids want to be alike, yet different enough to say they do their own thing. That desire for a likeness creates the classroom dynamics. Before you begin using teasing as a friendly gesture, make sure you know which class will "get it" and which one won't, by listening to their conversations with each other.

Brainstorming Potential Solutions

So how do you ensure that your performance and your students' performance is in peak form? Here are some tips.

Review Your Journal

At least once each quarter, review what you've recorded in your journal. It will help you maintain focus, find solutions that please you, and solidify your feelings of satisfaction. If, for example, you find you repeat comments like the one about the distractions in a high school environment, you may want to consider either looking for another high school or moving to the college level of teaching.

Discuss Your Problems with Other Teachers

These are professional issues that affect you personally. Open up with other teachers about your questions. The things that occur the most frequently in your journal cause you the most stress and, by discussing them with other teachers, you will very likely find that they, too, have the same frustrations. What you do about yours will make the difference in your level of teaching skills and your longevity as a teacher, so give this due consideration. Whatever you do, don't just dismiss your problems and frustrations as the "nature of the beast."

THE PROBLEM I discussed a problem I was having—getting cooperation from my students to do what I assigned for homework—with another teacher. The response I received was to stop giving homework.

THE SOLUTION You obviously asked the wrong teacher. Unless you are assigning homework as busy work, then you must persist. Increase the value of the homework and grade it. Sure that's more work, but if there really is something to be learned from the homework, then it is important enough to take your time. In addition, do not accept homework late. If late, it gets a zero. Since most students are grade conscious, the participation will increase, as will the learning.

It's good to take a look at yourself. What have we learned now?

1. Taking a look at what you do and how you feel about it should be done regularly in this profession.
2. Have you performed the way you expected? Since you have set up a plan and have a track to run on, you can now do this.
3. Don't worry about reviews. They must be done. With your plan in place, and all your preparation, you will excel.
4. Have your students performed as well as you had hoped? Take a look back. A bell curve may apply.
5. Keep a journal, review it, and discuss problems with other teachers. You'll survive.

The Middle: The Teacher Who Teaches, Wins

CHAPTER 10

You're the Leader—Or, How to Lead Even When They Don't Want to Follow

You won't believe all the definitions that apply to "leader." Take a look in the dictionary to get them all, because your students may choose one of them.

A leader can be a short length of wirelike material attached to a fishing line on one end and a lure or hook on the other so the fish can't bite the line off. A leader also may be a guide or conductor, or a person who has commanding authority or presence. General Tommy Franks, Commander in Chief, United States Central Command, who made history with decisive battles that launched the war on terrorism in Afghanistan and Iraq, was humbled by leadership. General Dwight D. Eisenhower, supreme commander of the Allied Expeditionary Force in Europe, which broke the back of Hitler's Germany during World War II, and who later became president of the United States, said he just stood on the sidelines while the real war took place. Obviously, he, too, was humbled by leadership.

I heard a story about a teacher who, when flying to the West Coast for a seminar, found herself sitting next to a thoracic surgeon. When he asked what she did, she told him she was just a teacher. She said she was completely surprised by his response: he told her she was not *just* a teacher; he couldn't have become a surgeon without teachers.

What an awesome responsibility you have. You probably now wonder how you can possibly live up to such lofty expectations. It is basically simple. You just need the leadership qualities of knowledge, empathy, respect, and most important, heart. Coach Mike Krzyzewski, the highly successful basketball coach at Duke University, says this over and over in his book *Leading with the Heart*. And, if you are not afraid of failure resulting in potential heartbreak, lead with your heart, follow the Golden Rule, and you will lead your students to the successes they desire in life.

The Golden Rule: Treat Students as Adults and They Will Respond in Kind

That sounds a bit of a stretch for the younger set, doesn't it? Let's think this through. Adults expect others to respect them as individuals who have their own ideas, thoughts, and knowledge base. If you infringe on any of these you have hurt, or at least insulted, them. Children are no different, just less mature.

You want to challenge your students in order for them to grow in their ideas, thoughts, and knowledge. Instead of always saying that the stuff they listen to isn't music, spend some time listening to the words. You will find messages, some good, some not so good, but messages you can relate to your students. Then listen carefully to what they have to say about the music. Some will have given it considerable thought; others just like the beat.

No matter which student you talk with about this, always leave room for hearing their interpretation. Isn't that the way you want to be treated? If someone always shuts you off just as you start to give him or her your ideas, you stop giving ideas and, by choice, stop associating with that person.

THE PROBLEM I bring critical thinking into my lessons and follow up with questions, attempting to elicit the opinions that resulted from their critical thinking. I so often get responses that have no thought contained in them that I have just about given up.

THE SOLUTION The adolescent and teenager are struggling with trying to figure out who they are while their bodies are bombarded by biological and chemical changes. That's a lot to handle, so critical thinking naturally becomes distorted. Unless they respond in a way that sounds dangerous either to themselves or to others, do your best to accept their opinions as being valid. That is one of the elements of the respect you need to show for them.

Classroom Participation Techniques That Really Work

Gaining classroom participation involves moving toward student-centered learning and away from the teacher/lecture approach. Think in terms of the last time you went to a party. Which was more fun? The party where every action was planned ahead and you just followed along, or the party where a lot of games and ideas of things to do were in evidence, and the obvious thing to do was to choose among them? I have attended the latter kind of party; within a short time a group had gone outside to play volleyball, another stayed inside to play charades, and the rest congregated in the kitchen helping prepare the meal. In the former situation, everyone had to get involved in one game, so some just stood on the sidelines watching, obviously bored.

The No-Book Beginning

Imagine what you would do at the beginning of the school year if you had no textbook. There you are with this group of strangers who need to begin to learn a subject for which they have no official guidance. Start by having them interview each other as though each were a newspaper reporter taking notes. You do the same. Just start with any student (who will deem himself or herself the most unlucky person in the room to have gotten the *teacher* in this deal), and proceed to tell that student something about yourself and your family. It won't take long before you will get the same in return. Try to get to as many students as possible. If you can't get to all of them in one period, take another. This creates valuable bonding and building of mutual respect.

Second, when the books come (or when you pretend they just came), all of you have to start on the same basis. Ask the students to look through the book and suggest where to begin and how to best learn what they need from that book that year. You will be amazed how little direction you will have to provide. The interviewing approach has been done at the second-grade level with some minor modifications, so you primary teachers should not think it can't be done.

THE PROBLEM I began the year teaching without a textbook for an English class (that I had never taught before) by having my students, freshmen, write a paragraph about an event that occurred over the summer. I expected the books to arrive any day, so I did some Internet things, but eventually I realized the books weren't coming and I panicked because of my concern over standardized testing.

THE SOLUTION First of all, only worry about the things we can do something about. You can't change standardized testing requirements, but you can find out what they are. Once you have done that, make sure you are bringing your students up to the level they need to pass the test. Then move them beyond that level by acquiring one or more of the many books available for freshman English and using it for developing your lesson plan.

Group Study Is Good for Collaboration

Get together with a teacher in another discipline and work out a collaborative study. As discussed before, most elementary and high school students don't see the connection of one course to another. If they are studying Spanish they will, at some time, encounter the historical effect on the language. What a great time to tie them into a project with the history class or the social studies class. You know these things are all interconnected, but the young mind that has little concept of the consequence of actions has great difficulty grasping this.

The high school principal in a farming community referred to back in Chapter 5 recognized that something needed to be done because of the students' low standardized test scores. He added a class on tractor repair, integrated it with the language arts and sciences, and the test scores soared.

Motivational Techniques No Student Can Resist

Never forget that you are dealing with children. Whatever problems they have, they bring with them. It is only through maturity that we are able to segment our lives, leaving problems with home at home, and problems with work at work. You will not teach English, history, math, science, or anything until you have dealt with whatever is on your students' minds. By doing this you teach them to believe in themselves, to realize that they are important to you as people. Only then will they receive your lesson for the day. Just make sure that you use vocabulary they understand, and when you introduce new vocabulary, define it for them.

THE PROBLEM I tried grouping my kids to work on a project and the goof-offs did just that—goof off.

THE SOLUTION Select your groups carefully. Put an "A" student or at least a good student in each group. Also put a leader in each group and keep the group size to three. The so-called goof-offs will find they are pressured by the others in their group to "chill out."

Note Taking and Class Participation (yes, you read this right!)

If you are not quite ready to try the student-centered approach, here's another one for you. When discussing a topic or actually lecturing, you want your students to pay attention and participate in the discussion. Sometimes students at the high school age get so busy they really don't get enough rest, and so during the day they just want to be left alone. Obviously, this is directly contrary to your desires, so you do two things.

note-taking

First, you require they take notes while you are lecturing or while the class is having a discussion. You make certain to point out the most important concepts repeatedly as you lecture. You give them five minutes at the end of the period to summarize their notes and show them to you. You set up a chart with their names down the first column. Then across the top you enter the date. You enter the fact that they took and showed their notes to you on that day. Use a check mark or dot or whatever you desire. If they are absent on that day you write an "a" in the column under that date and topic, but they must still get the notes from another classmate and show them to you upon their return to get credit.

The second part involves class discussion and participation. Move a student desk into the V if you use that seating arrangement, or to a space very near to the first row. Sit in it with your pencil, book, and score sheet on hand. Read aloud the piece that you asked them to read for homework, and begin asking questions to elicit hand raising and participation with well-thought-out answers.

A variation on this that really gets them going is to ask for a volunteer to come to sit next to you and ask the questions and lead the discussion. To get this started, reassure them that you will do whatever coaching is necessary, and provide whatever answers the leader may need to do the job. Whoever leads gets two extra marks (which is 200 percent if using 100 percent for every excellent thing done in class) for that day, which means 200 percent additional for their class participation. That will get their attention. After doing this only one or two times you will find it easy to get leaders who have studied the material and know the answers. This puts amazing peer pressure on the rest of the class.

When a student volunteers an answer and it is correct, you write a 100 percent grade in the spot behind their name in the column under the topic description. This will continue for as long as you want. The motivation for them to participate is that, for every correct answer, they get a score of 100 percent, which is accumulated with the other scores they get. They get a zero if they have neither offered nor given a response; a grade between 90 percent and 65 percent for an answer not quite right, but to which they applied good logic.

Once every four weeks you calculate the average of their grades and post it on their grade report through the use of an Internet service like School One (assuming your school does this) so they and their parents can see it. If your school doesn't use the Internet, post the names of those who scored 86 percentage points or better for this on a bulletin board. (You should do this posting even if you also do an Internet posting.) Then announce that anyone with that 86 percent grade or better is exempted from writing out homework assignments for the next four weeks. You do it in this order so you have a baseline of voluntary participation before starting the reward system. Believe me, this is huge. Most students hate writing out answers to questions from the book, but will study to get the answers so they can get credit in class.

Placing a student desk in their midst has two effects. One, they see that you are actually writing down their grade when they respond. Two, it removes some of the separation and, therefore, intimidation level for normally shy students. You will get great response to this, and not just from the kids who always raise their hand.

Make sure you let your students know which information is fact and needs memorization, and which requires logic. Teach them that logical thought processes are like weighing information on their mental scale. You show them the benefits and the negatives of something, and the logical results when the benefits outweigh the negatives. For example, ask the benefits and negatives of driving fifty miles per hour through a school zone that has a speed limit of twenty miles per hour. They will get the same obvious answers that you do.

You also want to help them make the connection of new information to something already taught and learned. If, for example, you teach chemistry, and begin the year teaching organic matter and then move into inorganic, could they make the connection? Or would it make more sense to teach inorganic first so they can make the connection?

THE PROBLEM I teach Spanish. Obviously learning a foreign language requires building knowledge rather than knowledge learned in isolation. By this I mean they must learn the basic parts of speech before sentence structure, and so on. Every time I attempt to move into a new area, they forget the one just taught and so can't learn the next step.

THE SOLUTION Revert to teaching the basics of English parts of speech and verb placement and then try the Spanish again. Repeat if necessary until they make the connection.

Play Internet Games

Suppose you teach social studies or sociology. You wonder how to get them to read the newspapers or watch the news so they know what is going on outside their own world. Maybe there's another way: the Internet. There are many games on the Internet that you can use with an interactive electronic whiteboard or with laptops if you can make them available to everyone in the class. The following is just a brief list of games you will find at *www.google.com*: English games, math games, science games, number games, social studies games, alphabet games, Spanish games, French games; Grammar Gorillas, Basic Skill Practice and Games, Quia! French Activities, Grammar Blast, Math Baseball, A+ Math, Kids Domain science games, PrimaryGames.com science games, and many more. I have used the Grammar Gorillas and Grammar Blast games in my remedial freshman English class. The students loved the games, and at the same time learned or reinforced learning of parts of speech, punctuation, and sentence structure.

THE PROBLEM I have tried mixing Internet games into my curriculum, but I don't want to use it too much because I want students to know and appreciate books. Once I started using the Internet they came into class every day asking what we will do with it. They obviously love using the computer and hate books. I'm stumped.

THE SOLUTION If you believe the old adage "too much candy spoils the sweet," it might seem that the easiest solution is to use the computer and Internet all the time, until the students tire of it. Unfortunately, this won't work with the computer. There is something addictive about using the Internet for them. Go to an Internet site for fast reading of the classics. These are sites such as CliffsNotes and SparkNotes that contain information like the old paperback "Cliffs Notes" the kids used to use instead of reading classic literature. Print out the notes for a novel you want them to analyze. Then take the class time to read the novel out loud in class, at least in parts. Use this method to show them how much richer the actual novel is than the short-cut version. Many students will "get it" and many will not, but at least you will have made the effort. Then continue mixing in Internet sources with your curriculum, because someday your students may get all of their information from the Internet.

Experiment with RolePlaying

We begin our American literature studies reading *The Crucible* by Arthur Miller. The play takes place in seventeenth-century Salem, Massachusetts. Paranoia and mob mentality had taken over the Puritan society, causing them to abandon common sense and their own basic religious beliefs in their persecution and execution of those they suspected of being witches. The play was published by Miller during the 1950s, when paranoia and an unrealistic fear of Communism swept the United States, spurred on by Senator Joseph McCarthy. Miller wrote about the witch hunts of Old Salem as a way to show people that they were doing the same thing in the 1950s. I have the kids take parts of the characters in the play and act out some scenes. We analyze the speech patterns but, more important, through the roleplaying, the students are able to better understand the focus of the Puritan religion versus societal need for justice in order to survive. They seem genuinely disappointed when it becomes necessary to move on to other topics. You can use roleplaying in various formats. The kids will be receptive to using songs, dance, or a game-show format for assemblies. The message comes across much better than it would in any lecture either you or a guest speaker could give.

Many successful coaches use roleplaying to develop true leaders and empathy for and understanding of leaders within the team. Coach Krzyzewski (Coach K) believes that, if you are to lead effectively, you must pick players to play the role of leaders who have heart. Dr. Norman Vincent Peale and Dale Carnegie, the famous motivational speakers, both call it enthusiasm that motivates the audience or the students in your class. So, roleplaying begins with you. If you have true enthusiasm and heart, your students will be unable to avoid becoming motivated to learn what you have to teach.

THE PROBLEM I picked the obvious leaders in my class to lead discussions of various topics. Since only one of them could speak at a time, when he or she did, the students who answered the questions or responded to the comments were the other leaders or the "A" students. How do I get the rest of the class to participate?

THE SOLUTION Once you have picked the leaders, give them the assignment for the next class. Pick students for each leader's team. Tell the leaders it is their responsibility to prepare their team so they will be ready with good responses. Remind them that a good lawyer never asks a question unless he or she knows the answer. Establish class participation points based on the leader's questions and the answers of the team. The team with the most points at the end of the quarter gets bonus grade points or some symbol of their success, such as certificates of merit or any other motivational thing you think will work. To ensure that the rest of the class will learn the points of all the teams, require them to take notes, which you then review at the end of class. In addition, give a notes test periodically.

Read Aloud—They May Just Love It

One presentation method that you should consider using is reading aloud to the class. Many good teachers have used this as a way to inspire and motivate students. I still get choked up when I read "The Raven," by Edgar Allan Poe. He uses magnificent poetic techniques to enhance the sound, and rhythm, and depth of feeling in this classic poem. Many an English teacher became inspired to teach because of reading or hearing the words of the literary greats. I see no reason why you shouldn't use this to demonstrate your passion. Who better to read those beautiful words from great historical speeches, such as John F. Kennedy's Inaugural Address and his use of anaphora and parallelism to emphasize the important points of his message? Put your heart and soul into reading Patrick Henry's speech in the Virginia Convention, where he begins softly and respectfully with "Mr. President! No man thinks more highly than I do of the patriotism . . ."

until he makes that time-honored statement to inspire—no, not just inspire, but fire up men to start the American Revolution—"but as for me, give me liberty or give me death!"

THE PROBLEM I read to my seniors and they seem bored. When I stop and ask questions or explain something, they just stare at me with that blank look like nothing I say is going to get into their minds. What can I do?

THE SOLUTION Take voice lessons. The vocal cords and throat are like the curled brass tubing of the French horn. The real sound comes from your diaphragm. You must either not have enough volume to your voice or not enough true expression. It's your passion they need to hear. Once you have learned how to project your voice and feeling, you may also want to have them take notes, especially during the times you speak something slow and loud, or when you stop to explain. Include these notes in the periodic notes test.

The Mini-Lesson Works

When you notice a majority of the class having difficulty with a particular concept or idea, break up the class by interjecting the mini-lesson. This is a lesson designed to reteach or reinforce a message by way of a brief explanation or demonstration aimed at the observed problem. For example, during an overall lesson on writing research papers, I noticed from the students' writing attempts that many had difficulty properly blending parentheticals into their paper. I found a very clear explanation and example for them. When they were to begin rewriting their papers, I interjected this mini-lesson to refresh them on this skill.

Mini-lessons don't have to be given in the middle of a bigger lesson. You can do them at the beginning or end of class, as seems best. You also don't need to involve the entire class if only a few students need help. While the others work on a project, you can form a small circle of desks for those students who need the help, and sit with them to explain. Then send them back to their work.

THE PROBLEM How do I get my students to find the best materials from a reading to use for their parentheticals?

THE SOLUTION Always read excerpts from the readings that illustrate points you want to make. In most classic novels, scientific texts, or history books there are many good examples you can point out without doing the assignment for them. Most students need lots of examples when they are first learning how to blend information from something they are reading into their papers.

Use Demonstrations

Most science teachers have been doing this for years. If you teach English or creative writing or any class in which good writing is the subject, you too can use this technique. Many times my new students ask how many times I revised a book before publication. When I answered that it varied from six to ten and sometimes more, they fell into amazed disbelief. What better way to show what it takes to develop a good piece of writing than to take something you have written and rewrite it right before their eyes? That should dispel some of their fantastic ideas, brought on by the movie and TV industry, of how a poet or novel writer shreds paper in fits of anger and frustration. Okay, some may actually do that, but it suits the dramatic element more than it does reality.

You math teachers can work out a problem showing likely possibilities of a geometric proof. Let them ask questions as you proceed. Most students have never watched a competent adult at work on things like this.

How to Get Students to Do Homework

You will hear horror stories from kids about how much homework they have these days. If you listen to them very carefully, what you will hear is that they have homework that serves no purpose. They see it as annoying busywork.

Now that you know the real basis of the complaint, it is obvious what you must do to get them to do your homework assignments. Having said that, keep in mind that no matter how hard you try, you will still have some lazy dissenters. Don't worry about them. They'll grow up some day.

As your first step toward gaining not only their cooperation, but also their desire to do your homework assignment, tell them that you believe homework serves several purposes. They are as follows:

1. Demonstrates their ability to understand and follow directions. And it develops this skill through repetition.
2. Allows the student to study alone to understand a specific topic covered in class without the distractions of friends and other students.
3. Develops the ability to complete an assignment and report on it within a short time (or an occasionally longer time if necessary).
4. Adds to the learning of the material covered in class, which you will test them on at a later date.

THE PROBLEM I tried to be creative with my teaching, and let the students work with me out loud to try and solve a problem. But nothing seemed to get accomplished.

THE SOLUTION The key is responsibility. You must make everyone responsible for participating. Tell the class that you will grade not only their final papers, but also on participation. By grading their participation in the class discussion, everyone is responsible, and will become involved.

Dealing with Classroom Intrusions

You are into your lecture; everyone is taking notes, and in walks the principal with a visitor she wants you to meet. Ever happen to you? You tell the class to begin reading a short story or to work the math problems, or review the organic chemistry formulas you covered last class, and you welcome the guest. The visit, while very important, has totally disrupted your class. You decide to talk to the principal in private about the intrusion and ask why the matter couldn't have been taken care of another time. Now your lesson plans are messed up. What do you do?

Consider this alternative scenario. You have spent the better part of the class preparing groups to handle a problem, write a report, and give the answer to the rest of the class. At just the point when they should begin deliberations, in walks the principal with a visitor she wants you to meet. The groups have begun their work so you welcome the visitors, pull a couple of chairs next to your desk, and have a productive visit. The class barely notices either the visitors or the fact that you held a meeting while they worked.

Which sounds better? You know intrusions will occur from time to time, whether caused by visitors, fire drills, or assemblies. What to do about them becomes your decision.

Individual Student Meetings That Strengthen the Bond

If you can't imagine holding individual meetings during class without the rest of the class going wild and taking the opportunity to just visit with friends or do nothing in spite of the fact that you gave them an assignment, you really need to work on getting your students used to independent and small group work. One of the things you should do at the beginning of the year is have each student fill out an identification card or write a short paragraph of introduction as a way for you to get to know them. At that point it would not be wise to hold individual meetings to achieve that same goal, because of time constraints and the difficulty of focusing on one student in a room full of students you don't know well. But, later in the year, after you have trained them to work independently, you should hold these meetings to discuss progress and any problems, suggest outside reading that they will enjoy, or just to pat them on the back.

The inner-city school with huge disciplinary problems rooted in poverty, gang violence, and the like will no doubt require a lot of work in order to reorganize the classrooms into functioning, independent learning spaces. If you have just entered the teaching profession and find yourself in one of these schools, you will need the support of the principal. I believe you will get it because the principal will desperately want to change the disastrous community of the dysfunctional school, but may not know where to begin. Your response is, "Begin with me."

THE PROBLEM The kids in my school just have no motivation. Their families, such as they are, live on welfare, or are involved in illegal activities, or are in prison, or work at minimum-wage jobs with no hope. I don't even know where to start.

THE SOLUTION Start by developing trust. The majority of your students have blocked out learning because of fear. Their fear can come from the usual peer pressure, but more than likely comes from inner fear for their own survival and of winding up just like the rest of their family and friends. Your educated reaction to this is to tell them they will have a basis for hope if they have a good education. You can't start there, though. First you must discover the basis of each of their fears. Contact local law enforcement people, counselors, parole officers, employers (of the parents of your students), other teachers, and anyone who knows the socioeconomic environment to establish your information base. You cannot help them overcome their fear until you know what it is. Then, when they feel your true empathy, you can begin to build trust and begin to teach.

Class Dynamics—and How to Manipulate Them

Every class presents a different group of individuals with different temperaments, backgrounds, and levels of intelligence. Some are much more social than others. Some seem to have contracted a sleeping sickness. Whatever the differences, they are real and you need to tune in to them as soon as possible.

Should you expect to get all the "bad apples" in one class and average students in another and the great performers in yet another? Absolutely not! Most schools split the classes alphabetically first and then begin shuffling the kids around to accommodate the classes each wants or needs to take. The end result should be an eclectic bunch of rascals, all of whom you must teach the same thing. In actuality, while they are eclectic, kids tend to fall into friendly groups based on personalities, much the same as adults. So, in spite of the random selection process, some classes will seem filled with lethargy while others are on top of everything. I wish I had an explanation for that, but I don't. It is good that the students are mixed in the classes because that teaches them how to get along with people of different backgrounds. Your problem, however, is that you have a curriculum that requires you to get all of them through the same material and lessons. The students will challenge you because one class will ask different questions than does another class studying the same subject.

Dance or sing or use songs for the lethargic ones and do more lecturing to the others, but tell them all the same thing. The passion you need to show when reading for the lethargic ones is much greater than for the others. You must become multitalented in the field of presentation. Use more visual aids in the slower class, for example.

THE PROBLEM I want to teach based upon my lesson plan, but some of the students are too slow to follow, and some become bored because they are above average.

THE SOLUTION Everyone is different in some way. You could slow the pace for the slow learners and risk having discipline problems with the rest. You could speed things up and risk most of the students falling behind and becoming frustrated. Find out who the slow and fast learners are as early in the school year as possible. Focus your plan on the average student and place the faster ones in groups with slower ones so they can be in a position to help them. Fast learners will help others if their grade depends on it, so use group grades. This challenges the faster learners to give help to the slower ones.

Parental Participation: It All Begins with a Questionnaire

Do you have any idea what the parents read or what they know about the reading ability of their children? You may wonder why you should ask that question. The answer is that if your students can't read, a vast world of information and potential for learning is not available to them. You have to start somewhere to lead these students of yours toward an education. The place to begin is within the home.

Make up a questionnaire to communicate to the parents or guardians. Preface it by stating that the questions have been used from third grade on in some schools, and they provide great insight into not only the reading capability of the student, but the awareness of it by the parent. In addition to questions about the student's reading, ask questions about the reading that goes on in the family. It will tell volumes about the child's learning preferences. The following are some questions to ask:

- Does your child show an interest in reading? For example, does he or she choose to read other than when it is required?
- Does your child read for a sustained period?
- How does your child show any emotional reaction to his or her reading?
- What do you like to read? Examples would be magazines, newspapers, news magazines, novels, manuals, etc.
- Do you read in the evening instead of watching television?
- Can your child read the books or magazines he or she chooses with little difficulty? And, what does your child choose to read?
- Does your child come to you often asking to help understand a certain passage?
- Does your child discuss what he or she has just read?
- How does your child figure out the meaning of a word just read but not understood?
- Does your child read a manual in order to figure out how to either assemble something or to fix it?

THE PROBLEM I know that the response rate from the families of the students in my school will be miserable.

THE SOLUTION You won't know for certain unless you try the program. A non-answer from the parents could mean that they don't read, or even that they're illiterate, or it may be that they just don't care. Follow up with very kind remarks by telephone if possible, asking why they haven't responded. If you cannot contact them, use sample reading tests with the student to figure out their reading comprehension level, and go from there.

You can add to this list as well as delete some questions that are inappropriate, but I think you get the idea. The completed questionnaires from the parents will provide a basis for developing a real relationship with the parents as well as the students.

When and How to Make Yourself Available to the Parents

We have many ways to keep the parents abreast of what goes on in our classrooms. I personally like e-mail, except in certain circumstances, such as when a student's personality suddenly changes, or a student just can't seem to learn the material, or is absent a lot, or not doing homework, among many other possibilities. Most people have a computer at home or access to one at work. I have several reasons for liking e-mail. First, I can send or receive a message when I have the time. Also, both the parent and I can digest the other's message to determine the best response or solution to the problem before meeting. I have a folder in which I electronically file these communications on my PC. I understand from legal counsel that the courts accept e-mail transcripts as evidence if needed.

I like using a cell phone for the same reasons. Sometimes when I send e-mails back and forth with a parent it becomes clear that we need to talk. I give them my cell phone number and the best times I can talk to them without interruption and in private. I have yet to have a parent complain about this approach. Knowing I won't have written documentation of these conversations, I make notes while talking to the parent and file these electronically.

Letters may also work for more formal communications such as advising the parent when the student becomes a member of the National Honor Society, or when the student has done something extraordinary. These take time but, obviously, leave a written documentation of the communication. We need to keep the parents or guardians abreast not only of disciplinary actions, but also awards and praises. We should never assume that the youth carried an important message home and discussed it with his or her parents or guardians.

You must do this. You must also do it in such a way that you still get your work accomplished and remain sane. You really don't want parents calling you at all hours of the day and night; if they do, you won't get papers graded until the end of the year. So, when do you make yourself available to the parents?

Make the parents aware of your hours before and after school. If you want to contact parents during your planning period that's great, but be careful about letting them know the scheduled times of your planning periods. If parents start calling you then, you will lose that much-needed time during the day. You can make exceptions when a student is having special problems that the parent can help with. In those instances I even give the parents my personal cell phone number and tell them to call me anytime. Usually there are very few of these, and if you initiate contact with them, they rarely have a need to call you.

E-mail is a godsend to time management. You can set aside a special time every day to respond to these. That way, you can communicate without interrupting your other work.

Parent-teacher consultations will vary by class, just as the classroom dynamics differ among the classes. Again, schedule these for the morning, before class begins. Everyone will be at their sharpest, and the meetings will be more productive than they would be after school. Within the strict time frame of a morning consultation, there is little chance of the meeting going off subject and rambling on while the clock happily ticks along.

When **Not** *to Make Yourself Available to Parents*

As harsh as this topic sounds, the fact is that you must have a personal life or you will burn out. We need good teachers more than we need for parents to have round-the-clock access to them.

Close your store on the weekends unless the school has scheduled an open house, a reception, or some other function. This doesn't mean you don't work on the weekends; *au contraire*. There is no need to try to fool you new teachers into thinking you will have your weekends completely free for golf, tennis, shopping, or whatever activity you either enjoy or feel you must do (such as housework). Remember, one of your original goals was to work on grading papers for approximately eight hours each weekend. That pretty well takes care of Saturday, especially if you plan to attend the school's sports games or maybe even the games or activities in which your own children participate. Keep Sunday for your own reflection and rest. Those two things will recharge you and have you primed for a Monday that may bring disciplinary problems with bullies, or the class loudmouth, or couples, or the too-friendly student, and more.

THE PROBLEM One of my student's parents became very upset over a grade I gave for a research paper and demanded a meeting with me and the principal. The grade directly reflected the student's missing several specific required items. The meeting turned ugly when I told the parents I wouldn't change the grade just because they disagreed with the way I graded the assignment.

THE SOLUTION Without knowing exactly what happened or what was said, anytime anyone has become very angry, their good sense has left them. Make sure you recognize that. Speaking to parents in soft, nonthreatening tones and explaining the importance of the grading without sounding in any way like you're talking down to them is the way to go. Attempt to gently describe the big picture of the course involved. Most important, be calm and allow time for their ability to reason to return.

Let's sum up this chapter:

1. Getting class participation is now a problem of the past.
2. Note taking, Internet games, role-playing, reading aloud to your students, using the mini-lesson, and demonstrations are just some of the techniques you now have in your repertoire. Think student-centered to devise more of your own.
3. Intrusions into an active classroom are not a problem.
4. Classes or groups of people or kids are all different. You can now figure them out to gain ground in teaching and staying on plan.
5. Parental participation is always a plus. Bring them into the picture every chance you get. E-mail them, phone them, write to them, talk to them.
6. In order to maintain your sanity and focus, it is okay to have times when parents can't get in touch with you.

CHAPTER 11

The "D" Word—Discipline

A simplistic definition of discipline is "to train or develop by instruction and exercise, especially in self-control." This definition, however, makes no mention of external events and their potential impact on a situation. You must understand how these things impact your classroom management.

You read in the newspapers every day about how the world has become a dangerous place filled with violence and mayhem. Should you conclude that your school provides a microcosm of this, presenting you with the prospect of daily near-death experiences? Think about it, and remember what sells newspapers. You should not ignore the Columbine-like incidents, but do not allow them to become the core for your rules of conduct. Good classroom management will reduce your disciplinary problems.

It's About Seating

Welcome to that first day of the new school year. The unfamiliar school territory has frightened the new students, who are already confused and concerned about making new friends, and, incidentally, about finding their classrooms. The returning students for the most part actually like being back in school. Oh, they'll complain about the short summer, but they enjoy returning to the camaraderie of their friends again.

If you are new to the school the students will scope you out and decide early on whether or not they like you. That first day is critical for you. Seating charts and methods were discussed in Chapter 8 so now you will only be concerned with seating as it relates directly to discipline. Do not use seating as either a reward or punishment. At the beginning of the school year you make it known that your classroom is a place for learning and in order for that to take place you require respect for each other and for you. If you find that certain students can't behave when seated next to each other simply separate them without a fuss.

THE PROBLEM The kids are too old to be assigned seats, but end up disrupting class if they're left on their own to choose where to sit.

THE SOLUTION Let them act maturely. Allow them to choose their own seats. Explain the responsibilities that come with picking where they sit. If they fail to be responsible by misbehaving, separate them. When you use interactive classroom techniques that keep everyone moving for a good portion of each class period, most seating issues and disciplinary issues disappear.

Explaining School Rules

At the beginning of the school year, spend time explaining the reasoning behind school rules. Do not focus on penalties for infractions, but the reasons for the rules. For example, my school does not allow cell phones. This rule has been in place since the invention of cell phones, and yet I still hear objections to the rule: "My mom needs to be able to get in touch with me." "What do I do if I have to call home, or we get out early and I need a ride?" "How am I supposed to let my parents know I'm staying late?"

They ask questions like these because they want to test you and hope you'll make the mistake of allowing cell phones in the classroom. Never, never fall for that trap! I answer by way of explanation. We don't want cell phones because they disrupt class, they assist in cheating on tests with text messaging, and they have built-in cameras, which can only cause further classroom distraction. Explain that if there's a problem or emergency, there's a phone in the office they can use.

Remind your students to read the school manual so they know and can abide by the rules, because you must enforce them. A lot of thought and reasoning went into the development of those rules, so every teacher needs to provide consistency with enforcement to eliminate confusion.

THE PROBLEM The school rules are there, but my students don't listen to them.

THE SOLUTION When explaining the rules, do not focus on penalties. Focus on reasons. Kids are going to ask why. So explain to them why the rule is in place, rather than what's going to happen if they break it.

Focus on why!

Enforcing Your Classroom Rules

Enforce your rules, or the students will redefine them for you. The students you teach will grow up to live in a country filled with rules, or laws. The pledge of the Junior Chamber of Commerce includes a very telling phrase in this regard. It is as follows: "our country is run by a government of laws, not of men." Rules should be a part of what you teach, so your students will get used to the idea. Our country's laws must have blinders on and, therefore, apply equally to all citizens. So, again, explaining the rules and the reasons for them, and even letting the students set some of the rules, will render the rules more effective—but only if you enforce them. For example, if you say no chewing gum, then you must *always* provide the appropriate punishment for the offense when discovered. Decide the most important rule for your classroom, and use that as the basis for all the others.

How do you penalize a student for breaking that rule? Do you make him or her sit in the corner, take a time out, or go to the principal's office? No. Not unless you're dealing with a habitual offender. If I hear someone swear—no matter what I am doing—I stop, walk over to the offending student, stare intently into his or her eyes for a long moment, and then I tell the offender in my most stern voice that he or she has insulted me and deeply hurt my feelings, and to please never say those words again.

Stern, calm, deliberate corrections without shouting provide a powerful message, and do work. About halfway through the school year one of my juniors asked if they could call me Fred, my first name. By that time of year my students had come to realize that they could approach me on most any subject. I responded, however, much the way I do to swearing. I walked slowly to the requesting student until I stood very close to him, nearly touching his desk, causing him to have to look straight up to see my face. He and his buddies fought back snickers, probably from embarrassment, or possibly because his buddies thought I would clobber him. I stared at him intently, and then scanned the rest of his friends and the room before speaking to make sure I had everyone's attention. Speaking in my most stern voice, I told him, while again scanning his buddies with my eyes, that I considered it the height of disrespect to call me by my first name and it would not be acceptable. I gave them all a moment of silence, and walked away. They got the message. No one asked again.

At first, it's a challenge to never raise your voice and yell at a student. When the class has become disturbed by someone acting out, you need to calmly correct that person and, if the other students start mumbling, wait patiently for calm to restore itself. Your silence will actually become contagious, especially once they learn that you will have to cover the same amount of material in the shortened time frame caused by their disruptive behavior, meaning they will have to work harder in class and will get more homework.

When that doesn't work, you can try self-monitoring behavior. When someone disrupts the class and everyone begins talking and moving around in their seats, unable to hear you over the din, create the "watch rule" and just look at your watch.

My watch rule means that for every second I look at my watch, everyone stays after school two seconds. When the students who hate to stay after (and that would be most of them), or who have a bus to catch, see me "watch-staring" they quiet the rest, thus saving me from resorting to raising my voice. If that doesn't work, find their "currency," which is whatever motivates them or what they like to do such as to play video games. There are lots of educational video games they will enjoy playing so use them. As long as we treat everyone the same, we should not have to concern ourselves with spending time in a courtroom, our disciplinary problems will lessen, and the learning experience in your classroom will benefit.

Near the end of one school year a student told me he liked my class because I didn't yell at them like so many other teachers had done, and practically all of the rest of the class joined in with their agreement. You must not consider your relationships with your students as adversarial. If you get into a confrontation with a disruptive student, the student wins.

THE PROBLEM The rules are set, but how do I make my students listen to them?

THE SOLUTION Never yell. Yelling gets you absolutely nowhere. Approach the student. Look them sternly in the eye. Then deliver a stern response as to why you have stopped class.

Dealing with Problem Students

These are kids who may make you want to strangle them. But, of course, you can't. You may want them to pay an especially humiliating price for their actions, but you know better. Remember, you want to correct the behavior.

The Bully

Someone has probably already made the bully feel worthless. He or she feels the need to compensate for that, and often does so by acting out against other youths. You have to remember to provide fair treatment to properly manage your classroom. Beware of sending the offender out of the room, but make sure he or she does not completely disturb the classroom routine. A parent may file suit stating that your job is to teach all the students in your class, not to try to rescue an alleged bully.

Bullying today isn't just the purview of boys. Girls use the same taunting, teasing, cyber bullying, gossip-spreading, and physical intimidation that their male counterparts employ. Since social relations are just as important as education for kids, bullying causes serious problems for the victim. You must take a proactive stance in your classroom and prepare yourself to enlist the help of the parents. The likelihood that parents will notice their child has been bullied and contact you for help is greater than that of you recognizing it first.

There are many warning signs that bullying is occurring: parents call to talk about their child not wanting to go to school anymore, or having unexplained bruises, or slipping grades, or about the child's belongings being missing. Watch the kids as they walk the halls. That's where you will notice such things as one kid carrying lots of books and the others around him or her carrying few or none; teasing or whispering in close proximity to the child; pushing or shoving. What can you do?

Don't ignore it. And do not focus solely on the one who is bullying. The key to stop bullying lies in the victim. He or she must find the courage to stand up to the bully, and you should encourage them and find ways for them to do so. However, if it worsens or it appears that serious physical harm may come to the targeted child, get the parents and principal involved.

THE PROBLEM One child is always making school miserable for others. Do I just repeatedly punish the offender?

THE SOLUTION Bullies are the most damaged kids in your class. You need to correct their actions, but do so in a professional manner. The bullied kids also need guidance. You need to build up their courage so they are not so easily bullied.

The Loudmouth

Here's another attention seeker. A loudmouthed youth can totally disrupt your class. How do you deal with him or her without actually diverting from the subject matter of the class in order to quiet this person? Don't forget the very real possibility that this student just wants to be the center of attention, or has a hearing problem. The first time this behavior occurs, ask the offender to stay after class for a few minutes—you have a question to ask. The student may lose some learning capacity that day worrying about what you want and that's unfortunate, but will be worth it. When the student comes to you after class, look directly at him or her with a concerned expression and ask if the student has ever had his or her hearing tested. Say that you're concerned about that, so you will contact the parents to ask them about it. If the student does have a hearing problem, the parents will thank you. If not, everyone, including the parents, gets the message. It's a win–win situation.

THE PROBLEM One student's yelling out is disrupting my class.

THE SOLUTION Be considerate to the class, and the loud student. Keep the offenders after class rather than berate them in front of their classmates. Rule out hearing problems before explaining they need to act appropriately and respect their fellow students right to learn.

The Class Clown

Properly handled, this student can actually add rather than detract from the class. Sure, attention seeking is the reason for the class clown's actions, but that's what he or she enjoys. Put it to work. Anytime you have something for someone to do on the board, always try to get the class clown to volunteer first. You will be surprised to discover that one of the reasons for clowning around is boredom due to a higher level of intelligence. That intellectual ability will come out if given the opportunity, and that "trouble" student may become the best in the class.

THE PROBLEM No matter how many times I discipline her, one student keeps acting out in class and disturbing everyone else.

THE SOLUTION Give the class clown the attention she wants. Have her answer example questions on the board. Make her read out loud to the class. Give her some responsibilities, and she will not act out to get attention.

The Class Couple

You certainly cannot have the young lovers fawning all over each other. So, what do you do? If you separate them, they will start passing notes, or stare at each other with stars in their eyes and brains tuned out. If you allow them to sit together, they will be a constant distraction. You cannot deny those raging hormones, so you've got to go with it as much as possible.

I recently had a couple who sat close to each other. But with my student desk configuration, one sat in the front row and the other in the second. This way they couldn't even hold hands or attempt to embrace. Somehow, though, toes seemed to touch, elbows rubbed, and the guy always needed a pen or paper. Rather than banish each to an opposite end of the room, I just called on them more than others, and they knew why. They also knew they had to take notes and have a good response when I asked. As a result, they both worked harder and their grades improved.

THE PROBLEM The class couple are infatuated with each other, and couldn't care less about what I'm teaching.

THE SOLUTION Do not automatically separate them. Keep them on their toes. If you ask them more questions during class, they will have to focus rather than fawn.

The High-Maintenance Slow Learners

You have a certain amount of material that must be covered during the school year. So, what do you do with the slow learner? This student will either have little interest in your class and do almost nothing, or will monopolize your time by asking questions a majority of the class knows. They can drag everyone down.

One solution is offering avenues for outside help. Most high schools maintain membership in the National Honor Society. Members tutor their peers as their main service work. Whether you teach in the local high school or at an elementary or middle school, you can contact the high school chapter's adviser or president. Since you can expect academically oriented and talented students, you can also expect good results.

Alternatively, if you do a lot of exercises using groups, make sure you group slower learners with better students who can help them. Doing this provides the slower students with in-class help, and the quicker students with leadership opportunities.

If a student is on an IEP, he or she is already receiving tutoring. In this case, you need to coordinate assignments with the tutor.

THE PROBLEM One of my students has trouble getting what I'm talking about during my lessons, and is slowing down the rest of the class. I don't want to lose him, but I also don't want to harm my other students' learning.

THE SOLUTION One way to fix this is to find outside help. Another is to place this student in a group with some of your more advanced kids. This way he receives help, and the others receive a lesson in leadership and responsibility.

The High-Maintenance Quick Learners

Like the clowns, these students can become great assets to the class. Make their projects more difficult than the others. Give them leadership roles in group work. They may also provide the tutoring some of the students need. If you don't keep them challenged, they will become bored, and you know what that means—trouble.

THE PROBLEM There are some students in my class who catch on to everything faster than their classmates. What am I supposed to do with them?

THE SOLUTION Challenge them. Make their assignments harder. And allow them to lead their groups and help their peers.

The ADD Issue and How to Deal with It

Before I changed careers and became a teacher I had serious doubts about the so-called Attention Deficit Disorder

(ADD) illness. We weren't aware of anything like that when I was growing up, and we only heard of rare cases when my children were in school. Some of us probably had it, but the medical field hadn't yet discovered it as an illness. I have done extensive research about the possible causes and prevention of this illness. Dr. Frank Lawlis, a medical doctor and ADD sufferer, specializes in this disorder. He says ADD may result from the breakdown of family values, the growing environmental toxicity of our nation, distractions of various video games and television programs, or variety of viruses in our environment. However, it doesn't matter what the cause; it still remains very real (Lawlis, 2004). And there are very real laws that deal with ADD and other disability issues in our schools.

Originally, Congress passed the Education for ALL Handicapped Children Act (Public Law 94-142) in 1975. It was intended to help the states with financial disadvantages stemming from a low tax base compared to the others. In addition, it clearly defined the rights of disabled children to free appropriate public education. In 1997, Congress reauthorized it as the Individuals with Disabilities Education Act (IDEA), followed in 2002 by the No Child Left Behind Act. The 2004 reauthorization of IDEA (Public Law 108-446) mandates that all youths with disabilities receive a free and appropriate public school education.

By the 2003–2004 school year, 6.6 million youths (14 percent of the total public school enrollment) received IDEA services. Specific learning challenges make up the most prevalent form of the disability, and have accounted for the largest increase in IDEA services, increasing threefold since its inception. By contrast, the second most prevalent disability, speech, has remained fairly constant. There needs to be particular attention paid to the requirements of this act because ADD falls within its purview.

The manifestation of this illness comes in many forms, but most of the time it starts to show as lethargy, sleepiness, inability to stay on task, and inability to follow instructions. When you add hyperactivity to ADD—transforming it to Attention Deficit Hyperactivity Disorder (ADHD)—you add constant talking, fidgeting, and the inability to sit still. Think about the following illustration as a way to understand the problems the sufferers of these illnesses have.

You and your geography class are discussing the Rocky Mountain region. You have dropped a map down in front of the board to give the class an idea of the great mountains' location in relation to your own. You mention that Denver is located in the Rocky Mountains.

While you are using your pointer to show the location of the Rockies, the non-ADD student looks at the map, sees the outline of the states, and decides Denver is a long way west of her school in Ohio. The ADHD sufferer looks at the map and sees the states' outlines, but before making the connections you desire, she glances at the girl next to her and wonders why her hair is so red today. It wasn't like that yesterday. Or was it? And then she notices the girl is wearing green, but the shoes on the boy on the other side of her look clunky and too big. She thinks about how you are wearing that awful brown shirt she despises, and that you are pointing to something on a nicely colored map. This is the problem with teaching the ADHD sufferer.

We not only have to remain ever cognizant of students suffering from this disorder to effectively provide them with a learning experience, but we must be aware of the legal implications of the application of this IDEA Part B because through its provisions, most ADD and ADHD sufferers have been put on an Individualized Education Program (IEP) with which you must comply. So, put on your finest patience cap and do your best to help these students focus. If the behavior of one of the ADD or ADHD students suddenly changes, contact the parents as soon as possible, because they may need to see their doctor to change their child's medication levels. Fairly regular changes in medication become necessary as the child grows and matures.

THE PROBLEM Everyone else seems to be paying attention to my lesson, except the ADD student. What's her problem? Why won't she just sit still and pay attention?

THE SOLUTION Know the disease you're dealing with. Familiarize yourself with ADD and ADHD.

Legal Conundrums

You might as well start at the source of what motivates much of our society today—lawsuits. Can anyone sue you? Yes, of course anyone can sue. That doesn't mean they have a case, it just means you have to defend yourself, which, obviously, means you incur an expense to prove the legal propriety of your actions. Did you unfairly discriminate? Did you think you applied discipline, but parents interpreted it as battery? When you hugged a youth to provide comfort, did you commit sexual harassment? Yes, parents have filed lawsuits against their child's former teachers on all of these bases. Do all parents have the financial ability to sue? They either have the money or can find it somewhere (Elson, 1978). We're teachers, not lawyers.

Be a Teacher, Not a Lawyer

In a case recently heard but not yet settled as of the date of this writing, several teachers had to spend upwards of forty-five minutes each providing depositions defending themselves against an allegation that they hadn't met the student's Individualized Education Program (IEP) requirements. In order for the teachers to have lost this case, there would have to have been evidence that they did not fully meet the student's IEP. They would have had to have shown no neglect on their part. But, unfortunately, that doesn't address legal expenses, which in most states would have been paid by both parties to the action regardless of the outcome.

The classroom should not be run like a courtroom. It should run on respect. Everyone deserves respect. It doesn't matter the age or category of student, or teacher, or administrator, or coach, or cafeteria worker, or whoever. All human beings deserve respect. So, you must establish your definition of respect the first day of the school year.

THE PROBLEM I feel more like a litigator than a teacher in my own classroom. I want to teach, and I want my students to learn. But I don't want to get sued!

THE SOLUTION Run a classroom built on respect. Make sure your students know you respect them, and they are to respect you and each other.

Don't Touch

Do not touch the students. I know the sweet, darling kindergartners and younger elementary school students really need a good hug occasionally, and so will a teen, but in the real world where a good child abuse or teacher pedophilia story makes great news, you become a legal target when you touch. These issues can come from unbelievable places and also include verbal abuse as well as physical. I repeat: Do not touch the students.

THE PROBLEM Some days I see one of my students is down and I want to give them a hug.

THE SOLUTION Unfortunately, nowadays a good teacher scandal sells newspapers. So, no touching! Try to lift their spirits with your words, not hands.

Don't Threaten

Those of you who have children already can answer this question. What do kids do when you tell them, "Don't you do that again!" Right! They do it again. They hear the word "again" and become so curious about what will happen if they do it again that they can't help themselves!

Shouldn't kids respond well to doing what we want when we tell them they will get a candy bar once they complete every assignment? Of course they will, but that will spoil them. Or, suppose you tell your class just before entering the museum that anyone talking too loud or getting out of line will get two days' detention. Will everyone then behave the way you want? Probably not.

What do you do when that unruly student challenges you directly? First of all, you've given this student too much attention already if you've reached that point. Now you find yourself caught in a power struggle. Step back and clear your head, especially of the anger and desire for revenge, and get the big picture back; the picture of where you wanted to guide this class this year. Now realize that this problem is just a very small interruption in the process of achieving the bigger picture. Treat it as such. Tell the offending student as gently as possible that his action, and now yours, have detracted from the goals of the class, and so the class should move on. Turn and slowly move away from the student as you return to the subject. This removes any physical threat he may have felt and eliminates the cause of the action.

The point is that you should never offer bribes or threaten punishment. You explained the rules at the beginning of the year and you always expect the students to obey those rules, not because you are "big and bad" and they should fear you, but because the rules are necessary for maintaining an environment conducive to learning for everyone.

THE PROBLEM Sometimes I get so angry with my class that all I want to do is yell "Shut up!" or threaten to send everyone to the principal's office.

solution on following page

THE SOLUTION Angry threats solve nothing. In fact, they cause bigger problems. Take a second, evaluate the situation, and respond like an adult. Do not threaten. Do not bribe. Simply explain and eliminate the problem.

Dos and Don'ts on Friendships with Students

"The virtue of self-restraint—or at least the decision to give special emphasis to it—has historically been preached by those with a decidedly dark view of human nature, from Saint Augustine to the present day."—Kohn

Every teacher has students who want to consider the teacher as their friend. They will interpret every gesture as a friendship overture. For the teacher, this is a lawsuit waiting to happen. Friends can more easily offend each other, especially at a tender young age at which they actually haven't developed a true sense of the meaning of friendship. Once the student feels hurt, you have a potential legal problem due to the student's misunderstanding your comments or gestures as friendship. The child's family may even think of it as abuse.

Tell this type of student that you, indeed, want to be *friendly*, but cannot be a *friend*. Psychologists give various reasons for this attention-seeking behavior. Some say that perhaps another student labeled this youth as the teacher's pet and so the student, although hurt by that label, subconsciously feels the need to make it true. Or such a student may be feeling adult abandonment because his or her parents have gotten a divorce. Sometimes the youth suffers from low self-esteem, or his or her parents act as friends rather than parents. Whatever the reason, the child most needs to see you as the teacher, the person instructing, and, therefore, the person in charge.

I compare this to my many years of experience as a business manager. The most difficult situation for a manager results from receiving a promotion to supervise fellow workers with whom he or she has already become a friend. If adults have difficulty distinguishing between friendship and supervision by a friend, then, obviously, teachers will find it a tremendous impediment to instructing youths.

THE PROBLEM My students expect me to be their friend, but then feel extremely hurt when I discipline them. I don't want to hurt them, but I need them to listen to me.

THE SOLUTION You are the teacher. They are the students. You can be friendly. But do not be their friend. You will lose your authority if your kids think you're buddy-buddy.

Dealing with Discrimination

Someone once asked Coach John Wooden, the famously successful UCLA basketball coach from 1948 to 1975, why, when traveling, he rented a large hotel room with a king-size bed for Lew Alcindor (later known as Kareem Abdul-Jabbar), and regular rooms with regular double beds for the other players. Wasn't that discrimination?

Coach Wooden, like all the great coaches throughout history, built his teams on a firm moral base, making certain they had their value system straight. He said that basketball should only be a part of their lives, and prided himself in treating them all equally from a spiritual standpoint. So how did he respond? He told the questioner that Lewis was seven feet one inch tall and could not sleep well in a bed that was only six feet three inches long. The larger room just came with the bed.

Was this discrimination? Of course it was. But discrimination isn't always a bad thing. We discriminate when we vote, when we choose our food, when we choose a restaurant, and on and on. I began this book talking about treating the children with respect and expecting it in return. Improper discrimination may well be the quickest way toward destruction of a well-managed classroom. If the kids feel for even an instant that you aren't "fair," they will reject you and whatever you try to teach. That's why it's so important to establish fairness right up front. Yet we may accidentally discriminate. How, you ask? By not being colorblind, sex-blind, intellectual-potential-blind. In other words, we must pay attention to how we feel and react to each and every student as an individual, except when we grade their papers.

Periodically, I like to do classwork that requires everyone to have a computer. We have a cart with laptops on it for just that purpose. At the beginning of class one day when I wanted to use the laptops, I asked the first two boys who came into the room to go to the library and get the cart. I asked boys to do this because the cart is heavy and difficult to maneuver through the halls. That particular day, at the end of class, I had a crying girl on my hands. As it turns out, she was in the room when I picked the two boys and it hurt her feelings that I didn't consider her. I spent some time calming her and explaining my logic. She said she understood, but knew she could have handled the cart just fine.

That won't happen again.

THE PROBLEM I unintentionally ask the boys in my class to do the heavy lifting, and the girls to clean the boards. One of the girls called me sexist.

THE SOLUTION Sometimes we do discriminate without thinking. Make sure to explain your decisions. If your students see there is a good explanation behind the decision, they will not see it as discrimination.

Parents and the Law

Generally speaking, the more the parents know, the better. If you never find the time to communicate with parents, you invite the courtroom into your classroom. Communication is key. The message here is to document, document, and document. I learned this in the corporate world. You need to make a concerted effort to discuss with the parents how their student performs. No one wants the surprise of a failing child at the end of the year.

Recently a senior in high school plagiarized a test, skipped classes, failed assignments, and missed a make-up session that might have raised her failing grade. The teacher began sending notices to the girl's parents in early April, advising them of her failing grade. Both the girl and her parents met with administrators, counselors, and the teacher. Just before graduation, when failure stared the girl in the eye, the teacher received a letter from a lawyer representing the girl's parents stating they felt she had graded their daughter unfairly without giving her a fair chance, and threatened to file suit if the teacher didn't correct the situation. The administration caved and the girl graduated. An immediate battle ensued as the teachers became livid at the school board for its acquiescence. The state bar association investigated the ethics of the lawyer, and the school board defended its position claiming the teacher hadn't applied appropriate grading procedures. Who's on first?

THE PROBLEM I feel like my kids' parents are not involved enough in their children's academics.

THE SOLUTION Communicate. Communicate. Communicate. Whether you use e-mail, or the phone, or an old-fashioned letter, notify your students' parents of what's going on at school. And do not just report the bad things; make sure they know about the good!

The Way You Dress

I discussed the types of dress earlier in the book. I want to emphasize that we dress in nonseductive ways. The earlier concern centered on looking professional and not distracting the students with your mode of dress. Now you need to concern yourselves with potential sexual harassment possibilities.

Just because the kids (especially teens) have some of their underwear showing doesn't make it all right for you to do that. Wearing skin-tight slacks that reveal panty lines, or wearing a thong (that is apparent because your blouse doesn't cover your midriff), or a T-shirt with a vulgar saying printed on it will definitely send you on a trip to the courtroom.

THE PROBLEM I'm not sure if the clothes I am wearing to school are appropriate.

THE SOLUTION If you wouldn't allow your students to wear it, don't wear it yourself! Dressing professionally will keep you respected in the classroom, and out of the courtroom.

When All Else Fails . . .

When you've got a serious problem on your hands, communication with key parties is vital.

Call Your Vice Principal and Principal

When dealing with disciplinary issues it's always a good idea to keep either the vice principal or principal in the loop. When you finally do call an administrator, things will go much better if you don't have to spend a lot of time bringing him or her up to date. Needless to say, it is especially good to keep him or her in the loop in case the parent calls first. For more information on dealing with the principal or vice principal, refer to Chapter 15.

Call the Parents

If a student has been disrespectful by calling you something less than dignified, or spitting at you, or performing any other insolent act, it needs to be made clear to both the student and the parents how this impedes the learning process. Make sure to keep your focus on this becoming a learning experience.

THE PROBLEM I don't want my principal to think I can't handle my own class, but sometimes a couple of the kids are too much for me to handle.

THE SOLUTION Vice principals and principals are there for a reason. Let them know who is causing trouble in your classroom. Keeping your administration informed is important.

I can guarantee you that, if you fail to notify the parents of disciplinary problems as you see them progressing, you will receive a very cold reception once the pot has boiled over. Their reaction will be something like, "Why didn't you tell me sooner, before you were ready to kick my son out, when I could have done something about it?" Good question. Irate parents breed lawsuits. For further information on parental involvement, see Chapter 15.

THE PROBLEM One of my students has been completely unruly and disrespectful, so I've continually thrown him out of my class. He was suspended and his parents called and were actually mad at me! I was just doing my job.

THE SOLUTION Keep parents in the know. If you personally inform them of their student's bad behavior it will not be a surprise when he or she is punished. Also, if you involve the parents, they may be able to help change the student's bad attitude.

What to Do That Really Works— and Won't Land You in Jail

Your schools all have a written policy for appropriate disciplinary methods. If they have done their jobs right, they have covered all vicissitudes. Good luck. Kids, like accountants waiting for the IRS to come out with a new ruling, can always figure a way around a new rule. Good judgment must prevail. The Eighth Amendment to the Constitution states: "Excessive bail shall not be required, nor excessive fines imposed, nor cruel and unusual punishments inflicted." I certainly can't claim Constitutional law expertise, but I wouldn't take the chance that a sharp lawyer couldn't find a way around that law.

So what are you to do? As I mentioned earlier, find the students' currency, and, if within school policy, apply it, and apply it with consistency and without discrimination. My school has the demerit system. If a student gets too many demerits, suspension or expulsion results. Good, you say. Really? How about the effectiveness of suspension? Nine times out of ten when the school expels a kid for truancy, or skipping class, or failing to stay in the right part of the building at the right time, the kid thinks he or she has been done a favor. I fail to understand the educator's logic in supporting suspension. We take the recalcitrants and send them out where they would rather spend their time anyway. Their parents may also have serious problems with it. So, what do we do?

THE PROBLEM Even after being suspended, one of my kids still does not behave—and gets suspended again. He's missing school, misbehaving, and not caring about any of it.

THE SOLUTION External suspension is not the answer. This student needs to be punished, but needs to be in school. Make him come to school and do his work, but take away the privileges the other students get, such as recess and free time.

Here's a thought. Instead of teaching them that, if they continue their ways, they will get out of school again, assign a special teacher to gather their missed assignments and hold the students in a room in the school to do the assignments. The teacher could even tutor them if necessary. We might discover that the youths have become recalcitrant because they have a learning disability. Or we may just reinforce what we already knew: they don't like school. Wouldn't that be worth the effort?

Let's summarize this:

1. Discipline has specific meaning in the classroom.
2. Mutual respect substantiates all levels of discipline. Students must respect the faculty, and faculty must respect the students.
3. It is a myth that all schools are dangerous places.
4. We must not discriminate in testing, seating, speaking, giving tests, giving assignments, or in any other area. Just be fair.
5. We must work hard to comply with the needs of students with IEPs.
6. ADD affects each person differently. We must keep that uppermost in our minds when working with those students suffering from it.
7. Do not touch a student.
8. Establish your classroom rules the first day of each school year. Do it verbally and even post them where all can see, and stick to them.
9. A teacher cannot be a friend to a student.
10. Effective discipline means keeping the parents in the loop, preferably in writing.
11. Don't forget that bullies are kids. Don't execute them.
12. Don't dress in a sexually provocative manner.
13. Class dynamics make it difficult to stay with the lesson plan, but we must provide all our students with the same opportunity to learn.
14. Apply disciplinary action with respect and fairness. And keep everyone in the loop, so when they need to be involved the administrators and parents aren't surprised.

CHAPTER 12

The "B" Word—Boredom

Keep Your Students Awake

I once asked a famous public speaker what to do if someone in the audience went to sleep. He smiled kindly and told me to have a helper stand in the back and prod them with a big stick.

When I first started teaching I taught insurance classes for agents' continuing education. My seminars generally lasted four hours, and some an entire eight-hour day. I took five-minute breaks every hour plus an hour for lunch, and lectured the rest of the time. When I left the world of insurance and entered the world of the teenager, the principal asked if I thought I would have any difficulty with eighty-minute blocks of class. He seemed surprised by my answer that it would be a piece of cake. Apparently getting teachers to agree to the block schedule approach created problems because they had gotten so used to the forty-two-minute segments, and they had their lesson plans set up for that.

Many people have asked why I made the change in careers so late in life (I'm really not dead yet). My simple answer remains true today. I finally felt like I knew enough to teach. Sure I only teach English, creative writing, and public speaking, and don't get into science or math or foreign languages, so what could I have meant by that statement? I can best explain it by saying that I enjoyed listening to my grandfather more than anyone else. I spent many an hour talking, but mostly listening, to him, while he sat in his greenhouse making cuttings to start the growth of new flowers for his floral shop. What could he possibly have had to say so interesting that it held captive my young mind? He had so many stories that, no matter what problem or trouble I had to discuss, he had a story to relate to it that gave me my answer. I also learned a lot about plants and how to grow them successfully in the process.

One summer during my college days I took a course in nineteenth-century Western European history. The three-hour-long classes, held on Tuesday and Thursday evenings, went by so quickly I couldn't believe it. Everyone in the class found this storytelling history professor so interesting that many times we forgot to take a break at the halfway point. Can you imagine listening to a history professor talk for three straight hours and stay awake? I still can't believe it. He told us about the history as if he had personally experienced it. His enthusiasm for his stories became infectious. Many times he would have to stop, choked up by the memory he had just resurrected. We waited, watching, as he took a deep breath, swallowed hard, and slowly proceeded to finish the story.

I have said previously that enthusiasm is the key to holding the attention of your audience. Enthusiasm doesn't always mean showing brightness in your eyes and raising the pitch of your voice, or using animated gestures. It also means sincerity and feeling the necessity of telling your story.

What if you teach math? Math seems like such a dispassionate subject. Well, take a look back in history. You will find how mathematics helped mankind to solve enormously complicated problems. How about calculating what trajectory you need to use when starting a trip to the moon or beyond? Mathematics can answer that question. And the science teacher should have a world of examples of scientific magnificence in medicine, biology, and more.

You now wonder, what could anyone possibly find exciting about teaching Latin? Take your students on a virtual trip through the Roman Empire. All the other Romance languages have the same structure as Latin, so you can tell stories about Napoleon or Mussolini in the language class. But, you say, this may cause inconsistency and problems for the history teachers. I say that it would not only not create a problem, it should bring those teachers into it with you. Switch classes or do collaborative studies with them.

Today you have so many tools available to assist in teaching that there isn't time to go through them all in this short book. This chapter discusses a few.

THE PROBLEM No matter what I have tried, and that includes standing very close to the student, telling his parents that he sleeps in class, and asking him to wake up several times, nothing works. He has a part-time job that keeps him up late and he just doesn't get enough sleep.

THE SOLUTION Most people, including kids, can't sleep standing up. Set up a way for him to read his book and take notes while standing. He will either wake up so he can sit down, or he will begin to function while standing in your class.

Movies

There is one thing you can say that gets all the kids excited about staying in class. Announce you plan to show a movie and they immediately think they get the day off from thinking. Since of course you plan to educate them, you only show a movie to reinforce something you teach. For example, last year, when we discussed American literature of the World War II period, I decided to show the students a movie about Dwight D. Eisenhower and D-Day. It demonstrated a wonderful leadership message and, at the same time, Tom Selleck did such an awesome acting job that it introduced my students to one of our country's greatest war heroes and presidents. I remember Eisenhower as president from seeing him give speeches on TV, and before seeing that movie, I couldn't have imagined Selleck in that part.

After watching it I asked my students to write an essay addressing leadership skills, characterization, and what they thought went through the minds of Eisenhower, his general staff, and the soldiers of the 101st Airborne unit who had to risk floating down from the sky over enemy guns. For the most part the answers reflected good cognitive thinking, and good writing skills. They enjoyed the movie, learned something, and further developed their writing skills. Win-win.

Have any of you seen *March of the Penguins*? If not, get it. It is an allegory for human life because it represents such things as having patience and perseverance, taking that first step to climb the mountain, writing that first word to complete the novel, preparing for the worst and hoping for the best. All of this is accomplished by the emperor penguin.

At first I know the kids all thought they would sleep through it. What's so interesting about watching a bunch of penguins waddle slowly over seventy miles of ice in frigid temperatures just to propagate their species? But as it turned out, not one student went to sleep or even nodded slightly. They absorbed those messages. Today's students are visual learners because of TV, video games, iPods, and on and on, so tap into that any chance you get. Fighting visual learning may make a few readers, but you will only win the battle to lose the war. They must begin reading regularly at home from an early age or, well, enough said.

THE PROBLEM I have a certain number of students who sleep through a movie no matter what instructions I give them before it starts.

THE SOLUTION Find out what your kids do in the evening. Most teens need ten hours' sleep each night but only get six to eight. Lack of sleep builds exhaustion over time, and a darkened room tells their bodies to catch up. Once you give the instructions and the movie has started, walk around the room to make sure they have begun taking notes. Periodically turn the lights on, stop the movie, make sure everyone is awake, and explain something important to the reason for showing the movie in the first place. Some may still fall asleep, but it won't be for long.

Audiovisual Equipment

If your school has the audiovisual equipment in a special room, you must have access to it or the equipment. Since the school already has this equipment, you will have great difficulty getting the school to purchase the same equipment just for your room. But, let's assume you can. At a minimum you need a projector, slide projector, flip charts, a lapel recorder, a thirty-two-inch color monitor, one overhead projector, S-VHS videocassette recorder, cassette player/recorder, laser pointer, TV/VCR, a laptop computer, and an interactive electronic whiteboard. Like that will ever happen. Right!

You all will come up short in terms of having all that equipment, but you can still dream, can't you? If you had all that you could show videos as well as movies, and interact with the computer. Realistically speaking, let's hope for having at least the TV (which will be provided by an outside vendor free of charge with the requirement that you and your students listen to their news broadcast once a day). Getting all the equipment can cost quite a bit, but it gives you the ability to show movies and hold demonstrations. Your school could buy one set and make it available to you when needed. One person could easily coordinate its distribution and use so all teachers could have the same access. Better yet, tell your administrators about the interactive electronic whiteboard.

THE PROBLEM We have an audio-visual room with state-of-the-art equipment, but I don't have a clue how to use it in conjunction with my subject.

THE SOLUTION There are a plethora of audio-visual software programs available. Go to *www.google.com* and search for software programs for high school or elementary school teachers. Your local university or even city college will have opportunities for learning how to integrate computerized programs into your course of study.

The Interactive Electronic Whiteboard

This device uses electronic imaging software on a laptop connected to a special whiteboard and projector. There are various types of these, such as front projection, rear projection, or a plasma flat screen. The idea of the board is that it imitates what appears on the monitor of the computer. You can show already printed material, material directly from the Internet, or download Internet material to your computer and show it. The whiteboard has touch-sensitive technology, so you can actually use it the same as the keyboard of a laptop. You can save everything you display on the board for future reference. The overall cost will run about $3,000 currently. But, don't let that price tag get in your way. I have an alternative for you.

Take a look at the electronic imaging software called the Quartet Portable IdeaShare. It uses eBeam electronic imaging technology. Because it's portable, you can easily transport it to an off-campus meeting, or to another classroom as needed. Your total cost including laptop would be only about $1,500. This unit uses the whiteboard you already have. Both units use special colored pens for marking on the whiteboard, and that means no more chalk dust. The following is a list of the benefits of this having this system in your classroom:

- Demonstrations work especially well for tech teachers because of the board's touch-sensitive technology, and these students generally like hands-on learning. It also has applications in many other courses.
- The kids all like color better than black and white, and you can usually get four colors of pens with this board. I use red, green, blue, and black. The manufacturer certainly offers other choices.
- Tactile learners benefit from touching and marking the board. Audio learners can go back and listen to the class again because of the recording ability of this system. Visual learners see what actually takes place.
- You can use it for all grades.
- You can connect it for distance learning (there will be more on that later in the chapter).
- One computer replaces thirty other computers in the classroom, as everyone sees the same big screen.
- You can use it with any software.
- Students with limited motor skills can use it because of the large area and the touch capability.
- You can operate the computer from your desk while the students offer suggestions and write them on the board themselves, which they seem fascinated to do in my class.
- Other peripherals such as cameras, videos, and the Internet can offer images to display on the board.

THE PROBLEM I teach at a private school with limited funds and I've been told that the state funding will not permit providing me with a laptop computer.

THE SOLUTION The regulations may vary from state to state. However, some states, including Ohio, provide auxiliary funds that will pay for things like interactive whiteboard equipment because it is considered educational equipment for the student.

Keep Your Students Involved

Obviously, the interactive whiteboard offers ways to effectively keep your students actively involved in learning. That is not the only way, so let's move on to other methods of student involvement.

It has been proven that hands-on experience is often the best teaching method. Although the lecture is not dead, just shortened, integrating the interactive into your classroom will invigorate it and stimulate those young minds.

While teaching book analysis and overall writing skills I require a book analysis once a quarter. I give my students the points I want them to look for six weeks before the paper is due.

During those six weeks I will have lectured on the basic elements of writing prose and poetry, and we will have discussed many examples of the use of the writing techniques by the great authors of our time. Approximately three weeks before the due date I ask them to show me their outlines so I know they are working on them and that they have the right idea for the analysis. One week later they show me their rough drafts, which gives me another chance to teach them proper analysis. On that day, after looking at their rough drafts, I divide the class into small groups and assign each group one of the points required in the paper. They have two days to develop their answer to that point and prepare to discuss it with the rest of the class. I recommend they prepare something in writing to show on the interactive electronic whiteboard while they speak. On the day assigned, one group at a time presents its findings. They give me what they want to have demonstrated in electronic format, a CD, DVD, or an e-mail with an attachment. I load their information into my laptop and display it on the board. They explain their display, and afterward I ask each group member a question about the thinking that resulted in their display, to find out if they all participated. They are responsible for both correct and incorrect answers, and everyone in the group gets the same grade. Obviously I correct any errors, so the class isn't led astray. The following class (two days later, since we're on block scheduling) everyone turns in his or her analysis paper. This grade exceeds a test score in importance, because of all the skills required. I also use other interactive methods, such as showing information from the Internet about the book. Sometimes there are interesting looks on some faces (surprise that I found a site they had also found) when some of my Internet sites appear on the screen.

There are a lot of other neat interactive things you can do, no matter which subject you teach. For example, put a quotation on the front board and leave it there for all to see for a week. Change it every week for the first quarter. Then tell the class it's their turn. Divide the class into two groups, and assign one half for the coming week, and the other half for the week after that so each of the two groups selects one quotation per week, and so on the rest of the year. Write their selections on the board. You can give them class participation points for their quotations. You, of course, hold censorship rights, and they get no points if you do not approve their quotation for that week. You can place any parameters on the type of quotations you want. No other reward need be offered. The competitive spirit will take over, and you will have a lot of quotations that are meaningful to the class.

Finding the identity of a famous person can get a lot of attention. Break up the class into teams. Each team has the responsibility of researching a famous American author or mathematician or scientist. Then each group has one of its members present the information about the author to the class, and ask them the name of the author. The class then has a period of time, usually a couple of days, to do their research to find the author. They will really work hard on this one. You can grade them and/or do something like give the winning team members school T-shirts.

THE PROBLEM I want to set up competitive situations in my classes to increase their interest, but I don't have the money to fund rewards.

THE SOLUTION Rewards don't have to have a cost. You can give extra credit grades to the winner or winning team or group. You can have the class create their own source of funds through selling things like school buttons, baked goods, and so on.

Distance Learning

This is where the specialty school comes to you. You just have to love it. With the right equipment you can bring some wonderful programs with their own instructors right into your classroom. This is not by using facsimile machines to transmit documents, or teleconferencing, or e-mailing. I used all of those in my former life in the business world, and only the teleconferencing technology is nearly the same as the technology now being used in distance learning. We held meetings in which everyone could see everyone else and not only hear or see their words, but their facial expressions and body language as well. What a great, cost-effective way to hold meetings with people from all over the country, without anyone leaving their offices. That world has reached our classrooms.

Imagine it. You and your class get to see a museum and have its curator take you through a tour while explaining the history of the statues and paintings, and then opening it up for questions from you and your class. That's way cool.

You need at least one video conferencing unit with up to 8 channels to allow for a good selection of programs, dual thirty-three-inch TV screens, and three cameras—one to see your students, one to see you, and another to see the room's whiteboard or other display. You also need a table with a microphone; a remote unit to control the main unit; and facilities including the choice of video inputs somewhere in your building.

This sounds like a lot of technology doublespeak. You really need to have a representative of a company that sells this equipment to come in and give you a demonstration. Basically this works through the use of several telephone channels simultaneously to carry a video and audio signal. You need a minimum number of two channels.

If your school can get just one of these portable units, it could be shared among all the teachers. Add to this Internet learning tools, and you will be working the cutting edge of technology to assist in your teaching mission.

THE PROBLEM The kids can never understand the value of algebra. I can't count the times I've heard them say they thought it was stupid; that they would never be able to use it in real life.

THE SOLUTION Contact your local bank or insurance company, if there is one in your town, or an engineering company, or manufacturer, or almost any business. These days many of them are using interactive communication equipment to hold meetings. Tell them you have interactive communication equipment and would like for them to provide examples of how they use algebraic concepts in their business.

Internet Learning

Previously I mentioned Internet games that could enhance your classroom teaching. Most of you recent college graduates already know about all the possible information that awaits you via the Internet. This tool can be brought right into your classroom through the interactive electronic whiteboards. But the Internet has much more to offer than just games. You can find the algebraic formula for anything you may desire. It abounds with scientific information. Go to

Google and search on your teaching topics. The answers you get back will be more sites than you have hours in the day to search.

The Sciences

The Internet has so much information that you should do some research before school starts to see if you can find answers to the types of questions that you plan to have on your tests. I bet you will. If you use this to your advantage by showing these sites to your class in an exercise for them to attempt to disprove the answers you find on the Internet, they will gain two things: practice in critical thinking, and that this information can be saved for study guides.

The Arts

There is a plethora of information on the masters. Use this to have your students research art history, and to see the work of the masters without having to go to a far-away museum. Again, most students today are visual learners, and this plays right into their hands, or should I say eyes. Why force-feed verbally when you can show them?

Last Resort

Stand up! Raise your hands as though attempting to grasp the ceiling. Take a deep breath and sit back down. If it's possible to summarize avoiding boredom, now's the time.

1. Showing movies always works, but you mustn't forget the purpose is education.
2. Many, if not most, of today's youngsters are visual learners. Go with it by searching every available source for both the equipment to provide the visual experience, and the programs.

3. The interactive electronic whiteboards provide excellent ways to involve your students and permit you to record their whiteboard activities as they perform them.

4. Today's youngster also learns well in general by hands-on experience so you should be spending many of your non-classroom hours searching for ways to accommodate this.

5. Industry has learned that with specialization comes expertise, and so utilizing the specialized knowledge that's available out in the world through distance learning techniques will further enhance your classroom learning experience in all areas particularly the sciences and arts.

6. As a last resort—no, better yet, as a regular practice—surprise your class by having them get up and stretch, march around, anything to get the blood pumping.

CHAPTER 13

Absence Makes the Students Restless

When You're Not There

Yes, it will happen—even if you just graduated from college and have the best of health. You may not get sick, but you may have to go to a funeral, or a wedding (yours, hopefully), or a seminar on a short-term basis, say one or two days. You might find yourself in need of some sort of surgical procedure that will take you out of school for several weeks. The list goes on.

With all your advance planning, you can just open the next page on your calendar and the substitute can work from it. Or, leave instructions on how to get to the next page so the sub can access it. I use a form I call The Substitute Information Form to provide these instructions. Either way works fine for the short term, but adjustments will probably have to be made for a longer term.

The longer term, unless it's an emergency, requires more work and planning on your part. In either event, you need to plan for time off before it happens. If you've prepared lessons in advance, everything should run smoothly. Actually, most principals or department chairmen require emergency plans for teacher absences.

Preparing Lessons for the Sub

You thought you had finished with all that planning you did before the school year started, didn't you? Surprise! Some things never seem to end, and planning certainly falls into that category.

You may or may not get your choice of substitutes. If you do get your preference, choose one who knows how to teach your subject. Choosing one who has recently graduated and hasn't landed a permanent teaching position in your subject could work well. You would at least get that all-important "enthusiasm" I've talked about so much. Alternatively, you could find someone who has taught for several years, but now only wants to teach on a part-time basis.

No matter who selects the substitute, the education of those kids in your classroom is your responsibility, and you must take it seriously. You must make appropriate preparations, leaving no stone unturned, and you have to lead the substitute very carefully through your plans.

THE PROBLEM The principal selects subs in my school. I keep getting one who has no inclination to teach. He just finds a newspaper or paperback book and reads while in my classroom.

THE SOLUTION Obviously, you can't keep him out of your classroom, but you can tell your students that a sub will be in on a certain date and their assignment will be written on the board.

Preparing the Substitute Teacher—Short Term

You have your planner or electronic integrated equipment established and have adjusted it daily based upon the material you covered in each class. You will have given homework assignments that need to be collected, tests that need to be graded and returned, long-range projects that need to be worked on, as well as daily administrative tasks, such as taking attendance, which need to be handled. Most substitute teachers will expect to find these kinds of things going on in an active classroom, but you cannot expect them to know exactly how you do things.

You should assume that the short-term situation will require a list of just what to do and what to expect. You can also expect that this teacher will not comfortably give the lecture you had planned. So, here's what you do:

- Dictate your lectures and download them to your computer, or dictate them directly into your computer, depending on the hardware you have.
- Have a list of information items on top of a folder for each class that contains any quiz or test you want administered, any homework or test papers you want returned, and any notes from parents about planned absences for their child. Also list other information, such as the class roster; the fire or tornado alarm instructions; lunch schedule; names of kids with special needs, and instructions for them; names of any diabetic kids, and the location of candy for them; instructions about how to contact the office, school nurse, maintenance person, and guidance counselor; the bell schedule; a copy of your classroom rules (or not, depending on where you have posted them), and a copy of the school rules and any administrative forms the substitute might need, especially for disciplinary actions.
- Have the teacher's annotated edition of the textbooks available on the desk.
- Provide instructions including user name and passwords to access your computer.
- Provide instructions on how to operate your computer and peripheral equipment, and a phone number to call for help.
- Leave specific instructions on how to use your computer to play your lectures and show the displays on your interactive electronic whiteboard. Also list the location of text pages for reference to your lectures.

- Have a small supply of looseleaf papers on the desk and a note telling the substitute the location of the keys to the cabinets, and pencils and pens available for loan.
- Write homework instructions in the usual place on the whiteboard in front of the classroom, and tell the substitute about this by adding a note on the list even if you have the opportunity to tell the substitute in person. He or she has a lot to remember.
- Provide a seating chart to help the substitute identify the students.
- Provide user name and password to access the Internet grading account if you have one. With this the substitute can (if you want) enter grades into the school's system.
- Place your class participation score sheet pad somewhere close to these instructions.
- Place a list of what and where you file everything on top of everything on your desk so the substitute will see it first.

THE PROBLEM I am never sure exactly what information to leave for a substitute teacher when I may only be out for a day.

THE SOLUTION If you want your class to continue without you, it isn't possible to leave too much information. Here's a list of essential information you can provide on a Substitute Information Sheet: names of children with diabetes and the location of some candy; the bell schedule, rules, and forms; computer access and operation instructions; information on accessing dictated lectures; the teacher annotated texts; instructions on entering grades in the computer; seating chart; class participation sheet; list of files; location of keys and supplies; and that the homework and the day's assignments are written in their usual place on the board.

Preparing the Substitute Teacher—Long Term

This substitute needs all the information discussed in the previous section. In addition, he or she will also need to do some actual teaching. This carries a different burden for the substitute. You need to do the following:

- Provide a copy of your annual plan broken down by quarters. If this resides in your computer, provide step-by-step instructions to access it.

- Provide copies of any future long-range project instructions, dates to have the projects accomplished, or steps toward accomplishing the projects, and when to supply these dates to the students.

- You should not assume that the substitute will know your subject well enough to teach it thoroughly. This is where your recorder and your interactive electronic whiteboard become even more valuable. If you have enough advance notice, you should dictate all your lectures and download them to your computer. With these, and the information on how to access and operate the interactive electronic whiteboard, the substitute only has to check your daily calendar, pass out papers, tests, and so on, and turn on the computer dictation along with the whiteboard.

- This one may seem risky, but if you want feedback with the voting peripheral that the students use with the electronic whiteboard, advise the substitute where to find these hand-held electronic items, and instruct the substitute on how to collect the data and e-mail it to you. This assumes you are able to take a look at the results and provide feedback to the substitute or students.

- You may want to continue to grade certain assignments. This obviously assumes you can do this. If so, provide instructions about the format in which you want to receive the information from the students. Depending on the assignment, you can have the students e-mail them directly to you, or you can provide a collecting box for these papers and instruct the substitute on who should receive this box, and how often.

■ Designate two or three students in each class to use the interactive electronic whiteboard, and make sure they know how. That way the substitute has a backup if he or she wants to do an exercise for which the plan calls for using that whiteboard.

■ Leave the names of a couple of trustworthy students the substitute may need to get the laptop cart for use during your class.

■ If you had planned a field trip, make sure you advise the substitute to have the parental consent forms completed and returned before a student may go on the trip.

THE PROBLEM I know I must have my plan data for at least the next quarter available for a long-term absence, but I'm not sure what else I should provide to a substitute.

THE SOLUTION In addition to the previously mentioned short-term items, make sure you break down your annual plan by quarter and provide computer access information if this information resides in your computer. Dictate all your lectures and provide directions as to when to use them. If you want to keep track of voting information, provide instructions for operation and access. If you want to grade papers, give your e-mail address to the sub, and also provide a box for assignments completed on paper, along with instructions for delivery to you. Before leaving, show two or three students how to operate the interactive whiteboard. And, finally, if you had planned a field trip, leave parental consent forms and instructions.

Preparing for Your Return

If your absence was short term, you just want all collected papers placed in the appropriate class folder you provided. If you have had a long-term illness, provide the substitute with some of your medical information, especially if you will need special care after returning. The children will already have a nervous feeling about what to expect upon your return. Tell the sub to let the kids know you won't really be up to full speed, but you are eager to return to teaching their class. Said that way, most of them will be empathetic, and will save their usual misbehavior until you are feeling better.

You need to make sure of your readiness to get back to teaching. Your physician must sign off before you return. Teaching demands a lot physically, and takes a lot of energy. You don't want to harm your health further, and you don't want to traumatize your students by collapsing in front of them.

When a Student Isn't There

The easiest thing to do is let missed assignments go. This does nothing to reinforce the students' responsibility, to say nothing about the fact that they missed a lesson. You should record all class lectures, input them to your computer, and, if possible, post them to the school's Web site. Your second-best option is to e-mail the lessons and lectures to students who are absent. The third option will become necessary if you don't use a computer. Provide the information about assignments missed to the student either through the school office or upon his or her return, and allow time for completion and return of it. You should also give students an opportunity to make up a test. I usually allow one week from their return to school for them to come in and make up the test. Don't give them too much time for this, or they will forget, and it will delay your returning the graded tests to the rest of the students.

Forms You Can Use

Substitute Information Sheet

Teacher's Name: _____   Room #: _____
Blocks:

Block*	Class	Textbook	Homework due	Other assignments due
A				
B				
C				
D				
E				
F				
G				
H				

* If on a forty-two-minute class time schedule, simply substitute "Period/time" for "Block" and enter the number and time of the period instead of the letter.

Tutor teacher: _____   User name: _____

Password: _____

Department Chairman: _____   Room #:_____

Annual Plan location: _____

Yearbook representative: _____   Phone #:_____

- Write new homework and assignments on the whiteboard; erase those due today at the end of the day.

- Office call button is next to thermostat next to door.

- You must turn on the interactive electronic projector as soon as possible and turn it off at day's end.

Students to get laptop cart or voting units:

Block	Student				
A		D		G	
B		E		H	
C		F			

Teachers in adjoining rooms:

Name: _____   Room #:_____

Name: _____   Room #:_____

Substitute Reporting Form

Date: _____

Block*	Class	Absent Students	
A			
B			
C			
D			

Note: Substitute E, F, G, or H Block for the above on those days.

To summarize the key points in this chapter:

1. Your absence really is missed by the students.
2. You need to prepare for a week out just as you would for a week of business traveling away from home.
3. Prepare your sub by sending any information we have on the school.
4. The better prepared the sub, the fewer hassles when you return.
5. Keep track of absent students and make your notes available to them over your school Web site.

The End:
A Good Teacher
Keeps Learning

CHAPTER 14

Managing the Paperwork

How on earth will you ever get through all this? Papers from the boss (the principal), papers from the department chairman, papers from vendors wanting to sell you books, test papers, research papers—and oh, some of those you can barely read because the print is so small. Without a doubt you think you will go blind before the year ends. But, you still have to keep at it, you can't retire for . . . umm, never mind, that is just way out there. You set up a calendar. It looked so neat until all this stuff started coming at you. They didn't tell you about this in college. You don't remember your teachers having so much—well, wait a minute, come to think of it, your teachers did always seem to have several piles on their desks, but you knew they were just unorganized. Ugh!

Okay, I wanted to let you get that off your chest. Feel better? Now let's take a look at all this paper and put it in order and go home to a nice quiet dinner.

Long Papers vs. Short Papers

Obviously, you'll be assigning papers of varying lengths. Here are the ins and outs of dealing with the different types.

What Is a Long Paper?

These papers range from a three-page typed report to a ten- to twelve-page analysis of a topic. Typically, the students don't do an assignment requiring a paper of any length until around ten o'clock the night before the due date. The libraries typically close by nine o'clock, leaving them with the Internet as the only source of information. They love the Internet, and it has become a powerhouse of knowledge, but it doesn't have everything. The next morning you get about two-thirds of the papers and one-third excuses ranging anywhere from my computer crashed, to my printer ran out of ink or toner or just plain broke. Or, and I really love this one, my Mom made me go to bed when midnight came around and I couldn't get finished. Or they cry, "I e-mailed it, didn't you get it?" Of course, it spent the night wandering around in cyberspace and never found my computer inbox. So what do you do?

You could give them all a zero for not doing the assignment. I have to say I don't agree with this. As you have told both them and their parents in the past, you want to see any paper the student actually produced as soon as possible. That strategy actually worked very well for me until this most recent year. In prior years I received 80 percent to 90 percent of the papers on time, and the rest came in within a few days. When the students who hadn't finished their papers on time came to me and explained, I gave them the number of extra days that seemed reasonable for the problem they said they had encountered. I told them that the extension of time couldn't go beyond the cutoff date I'd set to allow myself time to grade the papers before the end of that quarter. That all changed this year, when I received more than 250 papers to read and grade, and I had a weekend to do it. I had 90 papers with 2,500 words, or approximately ten pages each, plus another 160 various late homework papers of one page each. I had somewhere upward of 1,100 pages of papers to read and grade that weekend. Wow! How on earth can any-one do that?

After that semester break I began requiring all papers, long or short, to be turned in on time. Any exceptions must have my prior approval, and any paper that I do not approve in advance for late receipt has 10 percent deducted per day from the final grade on the paper, and this included week-ends. I now date-stamp all the papers that I receive. The Internet service I use dates all incoming e-mails, so that took care of dating any assignments I received in that form. Mak-ing these changes forced the students to speed up. The ones who had been late during the first semester either became punctual or didn't turn in a paper at all.

The majority now turn papers in on time. That didn't eliminate the number of papers I had to read, of course. That wasn't the goal. It did mean that, even though I could still have as many as 100 papers totaling 1,000 pages to read and correct, I would have them on my own timetable, allow-ing me to read and properly grade them well before the end of the quarter.

Your definition of a long paper may differ from mine, but the size or type of paper doesn't matter. The procedures just described will work for you, making you more efficient, creat-ing a more student-oriented classroom, and helping the stu-dents achieve a higher level of learning potential.

THE PROBLEM I just scan the long papers, such as research papers. I can give a composite grade and it takes a lot less time than read-ing every single word of every single paper. I also get to have a home life.

THE SOLUTION Actually, the way you stated the problem it doesn't sound like you think there is a problem. And, while you may be right, with your approach it would be very easy for a student to slip a paper by you using another student's paper that had been pre-pared on a computer. The other problem is the students won't know what was really wrong with their papers, and this greatly reduces the learning. An alternative is to require certain organization to the paper. That way you can expect to see commentary on the thesis in the first paragraph, the historical era on the second, and so on. Your reading goes much faster and you can grade each section as you have it set up.

What Is a Short Paper?

Again, your definition may differ somewhat from mine, and that's okay. You can still apply these concepts.

For discussion's sake, let's stay with my definition of a short paper, which is an essay with fewer than 1,000 words, or about four typed pages leaving adequate margins. These papers still present quite a bit of reading when multiplied by the total number of students in all classes.

You must read all of these unless a paper starts off so poorly that you can't get through it. It doesn't matter whether you teach English or a science or other course; if you require a written essay, the students should be held to proper grammatical rules. If you are a high school teacher, you should really be reinforcing rules they learned in elementary school. If you teach elementary school, you must use whatever techniques you have available to you, including those in this book. Our beautiful language is being destroyed by text messaging and e-mailing, and you can't allow that to continue.

Permit the students to rewrite and resubmit any essay as many times as they want. You check them and regrade them each time. You must be willing to reread the essays if the students are willing to rewrite them. Again, this is a lot of work, but each successive rewrite gets easier to grade because usually the paper gets closer to what you want. Have the students turn in the originals and all rewrites each time so you can evaluate the changes. Take a quick look at the original to refresh yourself on each essay, read the rewrites, and give the final grade for that paper. Good writing means rewriting.

An alternative to my total reading method for the short papers is to read a portion and make a judgment based on that, or enlist a superior student to help. Student grading usually will be tougher than yours, and it provides great experience. When it's time to return the papers, have the recipients meet in groups with the "A" graders and NHS graders to discuss the results.

You will find that the student graders tend to be brutally honest, and so you may have to remind them to put on their "hats of empathy." That helps keep down the hurt feelings. By empowering the students this way, they become more responsible. They also write better because they know a peer will see it and they don't want to be too embarrassed.

THE PROBLEM I just have to read every word of every paper I assign. If I don't do that, I feel I haven't done my job. But, I find I am reading nearly every waking moment both at school and outside of school. My spouse has objected, but remains patient and understanding.

THE SOLUTION By reading the papers as you have described, you must also make corrections wherever necessary and return these to the students and allow them to rewrite the papers, correcting the mistakes. Otherwise, they will just file them (in the trash) and will receive no additional learning from all your hard work. Sounds crazy that a student wouldn't read all your corrections or realize a lesson in them, doesn't it? By correcting only a portion of their papers, returning them, and having them rewrite the entire paper making sure they apply your corrections and comments to the entire paper, you will empower the students to learn and accept the responsibility for learning. You, on the other hand, will have only read a portion of the papers the first time through, saving a lot of time. When they give you their rewrites, make sure they attach the original. You can quickly see if they applied themselves to the project, and your total time spent grading papers may even be reduced.

Homework—Ughh!

They hate it! 'Nuff said. Okay, I really do have something to say about homework. You must consider homework as reinforcement for the day's teaching and not busywork, or punishment, because your students will resent it and most will simply not do it, and will begin to lose confidence in you and maybe even the whole schooling process.

The First Axiom Is One to Live By

If it ain't necessary, and is just busywork, don't do it! Homework, as you know, reinforces what you teach in the classroom. It permits students to work on their own, at their own pace, and, if set up correctly, enhances critical thinking ability. Always, always keep this in mind when doling out this work.

Second Axiom Is "More Equals More"

This one says that the more homework you give out, the more you have to grade. So use good judgment when assigning homework. Math requires a lot of practice for most students, so math teachers really need to have the students doing homework every night. Science has a memorization content that is usually best accomplished in a solitary environment such as a bedroom. Computer science is something that could be worked on anywhere, but, like math, needs a lot of practice. Language arts, art, and music have a memorization component and a critical thinking component that is enhanced through individual work. All of this means that you should plan on doling it out, being as judicious as possible to make sure the assignments aren't busywork.

Once you've assigned homework, what do you do if the students don't do it?

Not a Reward or Punishment System Anymore

You need to have either a reward system or a punishment system in place that is not connected in any way with homework before assigning homework. Your students will not hesitate to ask why you give homework, and why so much. Do not give homework as a punishment. The best way to assign homework so that it does not seem like a punishment is to start a lesson about whatever you want them to learn from writing an essay. For example, start a discussion on chronological essay writing (for any subject) about twenty minutes before the period will end. Worst-case scenario, you get hung up with one or two students who claim not to know what to do or where to start. Don't get far enough along to assign homework. Make sure you start at the appropriate time so you will run out of time. Just before the bell rings, stop everyone and ask them to finish their outlines and rough drafts for homework. Next class, check off students' names on your chart after they show you they have done these. Then you assign the finished essay.

Just in case you think you have enough to do to read all of these papers and to grade all those tests, prepare for the administrative paperwork.

THE PROBLEM I have tried stopping in the middle of my math lesson, knowing the bell was about to ring, and, when I announced I expected the class to work the problems at the end of that section up to where we stopped, many didn't do anything, and only a few actually did the right assignment.

THE SOLUTION Plan ahead enough to know exactly where you will stop. Stop with enough time to write the page number of the problems and the number series (example #12–#18) on the board as you explain the assignment. If you happen to misjudge the time and finish early, allow them to start in class. If it looks like you will run over, stop and write the shortened assignment numbers on the board.

Administrative Paperwork and How to Get Through It All

At the beginning of the year you will get lots of administrative papers. Not to worry—they won't continue throughout the year. You should read everything you get for the first few months until you start becoming familiar with the papers. Then you can figure out their degree of importance, and decide quickly whether to read them or toss them. The administration will need your attendance information, so prepare yourself to thoroughly check the rosters when you get them. There may be a student on the roster who may not even attend your school anymore. Set up your filing cabinet and categorize things such as educational information, administrative items, rosters, and class folders. When you receive ads about sales of books to teachers, place them in a properly labeled ad folder. Also place the school roster in a file, but make it a handy one because you will want to refer to it often during those opening days. You will receive a form that has to do with your professional development, attached to the school's development form. You usually need to complete this very quickly, so do that. You will receive forms to use for substitute teachers, so file those in your folder labeled "Administrative." You will receive the school's mission statement, the athletic schedule, the forms for taking leave, and usually a school directory. Again, file them all where you can easily identify and access them. You will also receive newspapers and magazines. You will be amazed by the number of newspapers you can subscribe to that will make you a much better teacher. File these also until you have settled in, and then take a look at them to see if you have any interest in them. You will receive a daily activity information sheet and an absentee list. File both of these. The absentee list can come in handy one day when a student misses an assignment and later tells you he or she wasn't there that day. If you have kept these absentee lists you will have one for that day and can confirm or deny the comment. There will be more, but, you get the idea. If you can't find hanging folders or manila file folders in the office or teachers' lounge, buy your own. Filing these things where you can find them is too important to shave a corner. You will need the same number of hanging folders and manila folders as you have classes, whether they are regular forty-two-minute classes or block scheduling classes.

One last comment on paper flow applies to how you feel when you see your desk. There will be times when you will walk into your room and find papers all over it. Don't panic. It may be that students brought in homework assignments late, and didn't know for sure where to put them, so they laid them on your desk. To keep this from happening again, set up boxes labeled appropriately and announce to all of your classes how to use them. You want a box for regular homework, a box for late homework, a box for regular essays and papers and other reports, and one for miscellaneous items.

THE PROBLEM That administrative flow of paper didn't slow down as expected. Instead it became papers on different issues, and the advertisements kept coming, just from different vendors. I'm still swamped.

THE SOLUTION Set up a spot on your desk for advertisements and another for administrative mail, or use boxes for this purpose. When you pick up your mail in the morning, quickly glance at each item for anything requiring immediate attention, date-stamp those, and place the rest in the appropriate place. During your planning period, spend a few minutes taking a little closer look at everything in each box. Pitch unnecessary items and place the rest back in the appropriate box. Once every two weeks, review everything in the boxes and throw away anything more than ten days old. If it's been around that long and didn't need attention, it won't in another ten days, so why keep it? File the rest in your filing cabinet.

Let's summarize:

1. Long papers are excellent tools for improving the students' writing, but an enormous amount of grading for you. Read only a portion for grammar, and make the students responsible for the rest. Group work on this allows them to learn how to rewrite and get the grammar right, and do the analysis you required.

2 You need to read short papers. Again, you can enlist help from "A" students and from NHS people to assist you in grading these.

3. Homework is anathema to a kid. Now that we all know that, let's make sure it truly does create a learning experience.

4. Administrative paperwork is big at the beginning of the school year and near the end. Make folders for everything you keep so you can find the papers when you have the need.

CHAPTER 15

Building a Support System at School and Elsewhere

The School as a Community

The support system available within your school consists of the other teachers, the principal, support staff, and parents. You need them all in order to do the best job possible.

Working with Others

By now you have figured out that you have chosen a field with a workplace consisting of quite an eclectic group of people. This means you must find ways to grow and improve your classroom management skills. You will find that you can grow quite a bit within the confines of your school's group dynamics. You must consider that everyone you come across has something to offer, so let's start with your colleagues, the teachers.

Teachers

All the teachers have something to offer you. It doesn't matter if none of them teach the same thing that you do. They all know the student body, the environment, and have teaching skills. Earlier I mentioned that a mentor could provide wonderful assistance to first-year teachers. However, first-year teachers do not have a monopoly on needing help. Even experienced teachers may find that other faculty members have developed new and innovative ways of doing or teaching old things. You may want to ask a colleague to sit in on one or more of your classes to offer advice on your methods. You also may be able to share curriculum resources, or sit in on one of the other teacher's classes to observe. In addition, you should attend seminars or participate in professional improvement workshops where possible, so it becomes known that you want to improve your teaching skills. Share what you have taken away from those meetings.

It's a good idea to offer your assistance to your colleagues as well as acknowledging their special accomplishments and in general befriending them. Avoid gossiping about or criticizing other teachers in front of students. Resolve conflicts in a mature manner and be patient with your colleagues, always treating them as professionals.

Many schools have begun using groups to arrive at decisions. Offer to work in these and, if selected, ask open-ended questions to learn others' points of view. Make sure you have a clear understanding of the problem before offering solutions. Be open to others' ideas no matter how wild or far off they may seem at first. Remember, groups have a rather short attention span, and easily digress from the issue under consideration. Find diplomatic ways to redirect wavering attentions back to the subject. Once the group arrives at a decision, accept it as yours and, therefore, your responsibility, even if it doesn't succeed in solving the problem.

THE PROBLEM I teach social studies and I can't get my kids to read even the local newspaper regularly.

solution on following page

THE SOLUTION Are your students taking a science class? Most enjoy it, especially the labs. Talk to the science teacher about some recent local incidents of fires, murders, or earthquakes, for example. Science in some form is involved in all these incidents. Perhaps you can have the kids write a paper on the toxic gasses emitted from an industrial fire.

Principal

Managing a diverse group of professionals and non-professionals presents even the hardiest of souls with daily challenges. Remember that information doesn't just flow from the top. Assist your principal by informing him or her of problems as you see them begin to develop. Don't wait until they have become crises before telling your principal. The principal should be your greatest advocate, but cannot fulfill that responsibility without your feedback. Choose your battles carefully. Make sure you have evaluated a problem thoroughly enough to know that you can't solve it alone before taking it to your principal.

Having said that, it sounds as though you should only go to your principal with problems. Not true—take rewards and small victories to him or her also. No one wants to spend the day hearing only bad news.

Take the initiative to invite your principal to your class-room when you have a particularly interesting lesson coming up. You should view your principal as an expert instructor who can help you improve.

If you take a problem to your principal, have a couple of solutions worked out to offer. He or she may see one of those as the right one, or may just need to tweak one a little to make it work. That's a win-win, and any good businessperson will tell you those are the kinds of wins you want. The support staff often can help you attain that goal.

THE PROBLEM I am getting mixed signals from the vice principal and principal regarding discipline in the common areas, like the halls and cafeteria. I am confused but don't want to cause a firestorm during a faculty meeting. Maybe it's just me.

THE SOLUTION Disciplinary rules should be stated in your school manual. The best way to clear up such a misunderstanding without causing that "firestorm" is to announce at the next faculty meeting that you are either confused or aren't sure about the application of a certain rule, both as it applies to common areas and to the classroom. State the rule and ask for clarification.

Support Staff

After you have introduced yourself to the staff and made sure you know where they keep supplies so you can get them without always having to ask, attempt to discover where their values reside. Not only do you want to treat them with courtesy, but treat them as professionals. Never talk down to them or treat them as anything less than you just because they may have less education than you. They probably possess skills, talents, and knowledge that you haven't had the time, the inclination, or maybe even the ability to learn yourself. Respect them for that. Keep them in the loop when it comes to any outside activities such as field trips. They will receive the irate phone calls from parents when a child comes home covered with poison ivy or a broken arm from falling into a gully. They, like the principal, can provide your strongest support—or not. It's up to you.

THE PROBLEM There are supplies kept in the office that are needed in the faculty work room, where there are several unused cabinets. For example, every time we need staples for the copier, or Scantron grade sheets, we have to go to the office and ask one of the administrative assistants for them. It would be much more efficient for us, and I would think for them, to have the supplies in our work room.

solution on following page

THE SOLUTION There may be a tradition to keep the supplies where they can be controlled by someone other than the ultimate user. Many businesses control maintenance of supplies that way because of employee misuse or theft. Maybe that was, or is, the case at your school. This is another good topic for the faculty meeting, where there is someone who can do something about the situation or, at least, explain the need to keep those supplies in the office.

Volunteer Aides

If your school allows volunteer aides, they will free up your time for more one-on-one teaching or reteaching, and will basically free you from many everyday classroom tasks. You have to take attendance, help some students get on the bus, supervise field trips, collect and distribute class assignments and papers; grade objective tests; find materials and videos in the library, make phone calls, and on and on—the list is endless. A volunteer can help you with many of the tasks on your "endless" list. Keep in mind that whoever you get to do these things will do them well, even though they may not do them exactly as you would have. People don't volunteer unless they have a strong interest in the project or school, so don't hesitate too much when thinking about bringing an aide on board.

The volunteers will need training, but nothing like the in-depth training of a teacher or a nurse, and will be eager to help in almost any way possible. If you have a choice among several people, choose one with experience if possible, but do get one. Keep in mind that the parents or guardians are another source of assistance.

THE PROBLEM I left my classroom with a parent-volunteer assistant and when the principal found out, she read me the riot act. I don't get it.

THE SOLUTION If one of the students in your class gets hurt while you were out, the first question an attorney will ask is, "Was the assistant/substitute certified?" If not, you and your school will be liable for those injuries. If at all possible, use only state-certified assistants or substitutes when you must be absent from your room.

Parents

I know that parents aren't part of the staff who work in the facility every day, but without their support our job becomes infinitely more difficult. Bring the parents into the loop every chance you get. I've talked about their support before, but in this case I mean their actual physical help. Use every avenue available to you to get to know them. The more you know about the parents, the better you will understand their children.

One way to involve parents is with a contract. Teachers use these most frequently to get the kids to do their homework. If the parent stands firm on requiring the child to take the time necessary to do homework, the chances of it being completed and done right grow exponentially. The end result will show an overall improvement in class grades as well as those of individuals.

THE PROBLEM I have a good student who works to his capacity, yielding B grades in my class. His parents push him to get and maintain an A average in all his classes.

THE SOLUTION You need to have a heart-to-heart talk with his parents. Be sure to start the meeting by advising them that they have a fine young person who works hard to obtain the B's and that there is nothing wrong with doing B work in your class.

School Activities That You Should Participate In

You want to do everything you can in your early years of teaching to become a part of and understand the school culture. Sporting activities, clubs, and extracurricular activities bring the students and their adult leaders together in a different environment outside the classroom. You need to see how the kids act when not in that type of controlled environment. Can you handle working with them as a coach or an adviser?

It may be fun.

When to Sign On as a Coach

You must know that many times intense relationships develop with the students in sports because of the time, concentration, and enormous energy applied. The players look up to their coach. They rely on his or her guidance. And, in return, they expect the coaches to look out for their welfare. Often that means helping them with making good grades and learning good hygiene and health habits.

The student-players see you differently from their classroom teacher. You could be filling the role model or mentor role in their lives. You have to make snap decisions as well as share your expertise. They accept criticism because they think it will lead to improvement. You have a great opportunity to reveal what it means to have heart. You have heart when you can dig deeper within yourself than you ever thought possible for the sake of your team and teammates.

Some of the players may not have the greatest home life and so will come to you for personal advice. The best way to deal with these questions is to help the student to find the answer within himself or herself. This doesn't mean you sidestep the issue—not at all. Rather, it means that you remember your advisory role and, through your adult thinking, lead the student to the answer he or she was looking for but couldn't bring to the surface. Handle these situations very carefully; remember, these young people look to you for proper leadership. If you think you can't handle that, but still want to get involved outside the classroom, take a look at clubs.

THE PROBLEM I have been asked to be an assistant basketball coach. I have looked at my workload and just can't find the time to do that job justice. I played basketball in high school and intramural in college and really love the sport.

THE SOLUTION Talk to your principal about it. You need his or her perspective on what you already contribute to the school to make this decision. It could be that the principal will want to change your teaching assignment to allocate the time for coaching. It could also be that the principal didn't realize the amount of work you already have and will withdraw the coaching request. In either case, you need that input to help with your decision.

The Pros and Cons of Becoming a Club Adviser

Most schools, especially high schools, have a plethora of clubs. The adviser should do just that—advise. How do you know when to step in to a decision-making process? The club members will ask you. You will see that they can't make a decision they need to make for the good of the club. They fail to operate the club. Otherwise, you should attend the meetings to make sure the students actually hold a meeting and stay on task as nearly as possible. You may also want to hold money of the club for them. I don't actually mean hold it indefinitely. I mean hold what they have counted and given to you for temporary safekeeping. You recount it in their presence while telling them you do this not because you question their ability to add the money, but because even bank tellers count the money twice. Bills often stick together. You record the amount and the treasurer of the club enters that amount into the club treasury records. You take the money as quickly as possible to the school business manager or treasurer or bursar, or to whomever handles the school's funds, and give it to him or her to put in your club's account.

The side benefit of being an adviser to a club is that you get the chance to know the kids on a more informal way. Many of the kids who join clubs do so because they have no interest in sports or the marching band. It provides them a way of obtaining social intercourse with other students with whom they may become lifelong friends. It also provides them with an opportunity to provide a service to their community, thereby instilling a community pride and spirit. It gets them away from the TV and video games and adds to the social skills they will need as adults. And one final benefit for the students is that it may offer them an escape from the boredom of solitude in the evenings if both parents work.

In the role of club adviser you aren't looked upon as the leader as you would be in sports. Rather, you are looked upon as a wise person, not a parent, to whom they can go for advice.

THE PROBLEM I advise the drama club at my high school. I wanted to give them stage experience, and so found a play I thought they all would like to participate in. I had difficulty with one student missing practice frequently and, because there wasn't much time left before the play was to go on, I asked a fellow teacher to take the part. Although the teacher agreed, he too missed a practice but told me very soon after that he realized he really didn't have time to do a good job and asked to be replaced. Although tempted to take the part myself, I didn't think I should take the role since I was the adviser, but I feel like I have let my kids down.

THE SOLUTION As adviser your role is just that, to advise. You add your adult experience when needed or asked for, but you must remain the adviser, even if the project fails.

Consultations with Outside Professionals

During the course of your teaching career, there will come times when you look at yourself in the mirror, and wonder how you got into such an awful situation. Nothing you do seems to work. Rest assured that everyone in any profession has those kinds of thoughts. Suppose you had a business career before taking up teaching, and you're thinking you should have stuck with the business world. You certainly made a lot more money. But did you get the same level of satisfaction?

One last thought while on this subject: You will, I guarantee, run across a child with a psychological problem not only beyond your expertise to help, but beyond even your ability to comprehend. Do what you can; contact the school guidance counselor, the principal, vice principal, the parents, or whoever can get the proper professional help for the child, especially if he or she is suicidal or homicidal. Don't try to handle that type of problem on your own.

THE PROBLEM I left a career as a human resource professional to teach. I didn't need a doctorate or even a master's degree in psychology to do well in that job, yet I handled many employees who had psychological problems. I see no reason why I can't apply that expertise to my students, or to any student for that matter.

THE SOLUTION As a human resource professional you dealt with adult employees within the parameters of your company's rules, with feedback from managerial professionals, and with readily available legal advice. You are now dealing with children within the parameters of disciplinary rules rather than workplace rules. These children do not have a fully developed ability for cognitive thought, and are entrusted to you for the sole purpose of learning your subject. You are neither expected to have the specialized skills of a child psychologist, nor wanted to exercise such skills. Leave that to the specialists.

Summing it up, we have the following points in this chapter:

1. Your school is a community for learning experiences.
2. You should look to your fellow teachers for help and advice and return it in kind wherever possible, no

matter their areas of expertise. You all have that common thread of teaching.

3. Your principal is your greatest advocate. He or she can't help you if he or she doesn't know you have a problem. Also don't just go to your principal with only problems. Take good news also.

4. The support staff keeps things running and is often the first line of defense with outside callers, so treat them as equals and pamper them when you ask for special treatment.

5. Volunteer aides can perform very useful tasks in your classroom. Use them wisely.

6. Parents can be your strongest ally next to your principal, so communicate with them often and well.

7. Activities of the students outside the classroom often tell you more about the person than anything that happens inside the classroom. Sports are a very big part of those outside activities. Consider carefully before taking on such a position.

8. Advising a club can be another good way to get to know the kids better.

9. Use outside professional consultants for problems beyond your expertise.

CHAPTER 16

Managing Your Career

Summarize your teaching process for the first year, or the past years, to begin the process of career management. Ask yourself how you feel about what you have accomplished. Have you done things to improve how you handle all your students' needs? In addition, you must give consideration to special needs children and the types of current and future learners you will teach.

Many students become eligible for an Individualized Education Program (IEP), and you must make sure you haven't overlooked their needs. Most students today fall into what the education community refers to as Generation "D," which specifically addresses the fact that they have become digital learners. That means you need to take a careful look at your expertise in the areas of electronic media and communication. Have you done that? You also should review your lecturing skills, your rules, and your continuing education needs for professional development, projecting the requirements of the future classroom that you will manage.

THE PROBLEM I have been teaching for more than thirty years and know my subject extremely well. I have my calendar all arranged and have been using the same textbook for several years.

solution on following page

THE SOLUTION You didn't sound like you thought you had a problem when making this statement, but you do. The students' learning styles have changed dramatically in the last thirty years. So how do you know whether you're getting to them with your message?

Child Development Study

There have been many child development studies, as I am sure you are aware. The one I have found that appears to make the most sense is by Ralph Gemelli. It is important because it focuses on the digital learner, or Generation "D," starts with the basic learning capacity development, and indicates four stages, all of which impact the classroom.

1. **Preschool stage:** where behavior and learning results primarily from whatever feels good or hurts; has nothing to do with instruction or attempts at education.
2. **Preadolescent stage:** ages six to twelve, where behavior and learning are instinctive but can be modified by reward and punishment.
3. **Early puberty:** ages twelve to fifteen, when sexual urges begin to surge. The child makes moves toward independence from the parents in order to head out on his or her own some day. Close friends of the same gender become more important than parents or teachers.
4. **Late puberty stage:** ages sixteen to nineteen, when the child begins to develop a real sense of who he or she is or wants to be. This new self must prepare to separate from the parents. Consequences for their actions begin to penetrate their young minds.

Obviously, as an educator, you must take into account these different stages and their effect on your motivational and disciplinary actions. When the child falls between the ages of about eleven to about thirteen, huge chemical changes take place. Because of these changes, this group of youngsters tends to say "I must" a lot. They just begin to understand the social implications of their actions, and can become very confused. (McDougall, 1926). It makes sense, then, that everything would seem urgent to them. You "must," therefore, make a special effort in attempting to understand how to get through to this age group.

THE PROBLEM I explain things until I think I will pass out, but the questions keep coming. The room is filled with questions, and an extreme lack of answers.

THE SOLUTION Here's where teacher patience comes in to play. You must take the time to learn the students' culture. You can explain something until you are blue in the face, but your students will still have a difficult time understanding if you do not relate it to them. Find out where they are coming from. You then will be able to eliminate the thousands of questions and, instead, receive thousands of answers.

Generation D (Digital Learners) and Curriculum Standards

You don't want to let technology become the only thing taught, but you really need to look at every possible avenue for bringing it into your classroom. After all, the workplace today is filled with computers, teleconferencing devices, robotics, GPS directional finders, and on and on. So where do you look for guidance to ensure you're making good use of technology, as well as teaching how to use it?

The first step, as always, has to do with the basic tenet of planning: finding out how to measure progress or standards. Setting future standards begins with identifying key skills needed for those standards. My crystal ball really doesn't work the way it does for those gals in long flowing robes (maybe it needs new smoke), so I believe it best to restrict this discussion to what we know today about this field. We know of five areas where technology requires specific skills:

Internet applications, hardware, programming, networking, and software. Let's take a quick look at these before going into curriculum requirements, which will result in changes needed in your classroom ("A Step," 2006).

Internet Applications

Internet applications evolve daily, with only a few having weathered the storms of times gone by. If you think e-mail is new, think about the fact that e-mail messages now out-number letters sent through the worldwide postal services by ten to one. Every senior graduating from high school should be proficient in using e-mail. File transfer proto-col (FTP) sounds like a fancy term but really means the use of a simple program allowing you to transfer files to Web pages. Future jobs available to your students require that they must have some knowledge of this. Your students should also become proficient with video conferencing and voice recognition technology and automatic transla-tions. Students don't necessarily have to know how to pro-gram these functions at this time (they will learn this in tech school or college or on the job), but certainly need to understand how they work. One or more of your students may have his or her first job interview in Paris in the com-ing months, and all that the student needs to do for the job interview is turn on his or her computer at home. Add to this the distance learning capabilities, and students can obtain specialized knowledge from almost anywhere with-out leaving your classroom.

Soon you can expect that the hard drives in computers will be replaced with online disk storage. Just a couple of days ago I saw an offering for this on my Internet browser. And speaking of browsers, there are four right now, and what you see on your screen depends upon which one of these you use. The student of today will also need to learn

HTML code to set up Web pages and know the abilities of each of the Web browsers.

THE PROBLEM These kids are so much faster on the computers than I am, I can't begin to know enough to make sure they have what they need.

THE SOLUTION You can't all be experts in the use of computers and the Internet, but you can be expected to understand them conceptually and to be able to navigate them no matter how fast or slow. Take whatever courses you can to become proficient. There are courses available at your local community colleges, and online, assuming you know enough to get online.

Computer Hardware

We have progressed from the quill pen, to Morse code, to the typewriter, to word processing, to HTML codes, to voice-activated communication systems. Generation D will continue to adapt changes to new needs, but in order to do that they will need to understand printer driver devices in order to print their assigned papers for teachers who want printed copies, and to evaluate the cost efficiency factors for the different printing technologies.

The world today thinks it can't live without hard copies, but even the legal community has started accepting electronic media as evidence in its proceedings. Hard copy simply takes up too much storage space, so we have floppy disks that have evolved into compact disks and high-density magnetic storage. We also have optical scanners, which have become very reliable. Your students will have to determine the efficacy of magnetic storage versus optical. Finally, they must know about the various means to Internet connections and understand the hardware items, such as the CPU (central processing unit); RAM, which is the random access memory unit; and the motherboards, where everything connects within the computer as we know it today ("A Step," 2006).

Programming

Computer programming began with two very cumbersome coding systems called COBOL and FORTRAN. Now there are many computer languages based on the unique tasks they were designed for, so it is impossible to know which language your students should learn. The key is understanding mathematical logic, so that's a good reason for them to continue taking such courses as geometry, algebra, and trigonometry.

Networking

This means hooking up two or more computers to share information and software. Sounds simple, doesn't it? It is as complicated as the diversity of our society. Recently I had a discussion with a physician who was on the committee to network three hospitals that had just combined. She is a neurologist and admitted total confusion as to why the three systems wouldn't talk to each other. Students today will certainly benefit by working with these kinds of problems and learning as much as possible about computer hardware and the software it takes to run it.

Software

The term "software" refers to the programs that make everything work. Understanding how software programs function is critical for teaching today's student. You should spend as much time as possible learning how you can use these programs also.

At-Risk Programs

During your teaching career you may encounter students who are at risk of failing state assessments. Be aware that there are assistance programs for these students. Two examples are the

Grizzly Advantage Program (GAP) in math and the Read 180 program in reading. Both operate on the same principles of small class size (no larger than twenty-two); double the class time (double block); student tutors; community tutors; extra progress reports; and frequent teacher/parent/student communication. These programs have shown tremendous results (North Central Commission on Accreditation and School Improvement, 2006).

You may also encounter other special needs students, including those with Autism Spectrum Disorders. Read all the literature you can find, and stay current on appropriate teaching methods.

This is not to say you must become a special education teacher, but that you should be aware that children with these issues require specialized teaching methods. You don't want to have that deer-in-the-headlights look when a parent tells you that his or her child requires special help. Know who the special education and tutoring teachers are in your school and where to send the parent if your school can't accommodate the child. Most school districts have complied with the requirements for students who have psychological and physical impairments. If neither you nor your principal know where this student should go to make sure all his needs are met, contact the school district or nearest city or state health department official.

THE PROBLEM I have a teenage student who dissociates himself from his peers. When class ends he waits until they have left before he leaves. I never see him walking with anyone in the halls. Most of the time while in class he seems distracted, as though listening to something other than me. When I call on him, his answer, although related to the topic, is a very different perspective than I expect. I encourage independent thinking, but his comments are so off-the-wall, I am stunned. I just know he has some sort of psychological disorder, but am reluctant to tell his parents. I fear they will be insulted.

solution on following page

THE SOLUTION Obviously you have a delicate situation, but you must take action. Have the school nurse examine him to see if he has indications of any sort of physical problem such as a hearing impairment. Based on the results of that analysis, you and the principal must talk to the parents, even at the risk of insulting them. You are a concerned teacher making a professional observation that they should take seriously if they want to help their child.

Speaking Techniques

You may not know that some of our past presidents and great orators used some very simple and basic ways to prepare for a speech. They provide valuable lessons you can use in delivering your classroom lectures.

President Theodore Roosevelt felt that you shouldn't speak until you had something important to say. Know exactly what it is, and then say it. Once it's said, sit down. He knew that no one likes to listen to any speaker drone on and on, not really adding to what he had already said much earlier. He also felt nerves welling up, even though he was sure he knew his subject. He called that feeling "buck fever," and found that taking some sort of physical action before speaking calmed him. These are two very good points you can easily apply. First, make sure you know when to stop talking. Second, if you're nervous, be sure you have a classroom with either a whiteboard or blackboard that would naturally require erasing, or a podium that you can move from one spot to another. The kids won't question such activities, and you get to calm yourself.

President Woodrow Wilson called his preparation technique "fitting the bones together." He would come up with a list of topics to talk about, and arrange them in his mind. He then wrote them down in shorthand. Once he had that document to look at, he made a typed copy, amending phrases and sentences and adding ideas as he typed. Next he went over that version, inserting and deleting and amending phrases and sentences until he had filled it with pencil marks. He then dictated or read it until he had absolute confidence in what he knew he needed to say. Therein lies our lesson of commitment through persistent reviewing of the ideas so that our enthusiasm builds.

Benjamin Franklin wanted his audience to remember his message, so he knew he had to sound almost rhythmical. He accomplished this by varying the length of words and sentences and using words that, when properly placed, sounded rhythmical.

Patrick Henry, one of our greatest orators, said "There is no retreat but in submission and slavery!" during his famous speech before the Virginia Convention. He wanted to inflame his fellow colonists to stand up to Britain and become a sovereign nation. His rhetoric was alarming because, in order to do what he asked, his listeners would have to be furiously angry with Britain. Yet he started this speech by complimenting the audience on their patriotism. He told them that he believed in the value of patriotism, just as they did. Then he moved swiftly into the fiery words needed to incite them to begin the revolution they all knew could cost them, their families, their lives and their fortunes.

So what did all these great speakers have in common?

Enthusiasm. Yes, enthusiasm, based on the firm belief that they were right. They persisted, using the power of speech to emphasize the importance of their cause.

All of these orators knew whereof they spoke, and that they spoke the truth. They prepared well through rehearsing, yet not memorizing. They stayed fresh by constantly looking back before looking forward. They had different things to say and used different rhetoric to say it. They knew what needed to be said, and said no more. No two speeches are alike, nor should they be, just as no two of your lectures should be exactly like the others.

THE PROBLEM I have a very soft voice. Many times my students tell me they can't hear me. I have tried speaking louder and moving closer to them without success. Maybe I shouldn't be teaching.

THE SOLUTION Examine your motivations for getting into this profession. If you reaffirm your commitment to it, then your voice-level problem can be handled. First get a physical. Talk to your family doctor about your problem to determine whether there is some physical reason for it. If there is nothing physical, go to a speech or voice teacher. Have you ever heard an operatic singer and wondered how he or she could have hit those high notes and projected the voice so well? It's a skill. You can learn it. You may not become an operatic singer, but your students will be able to hear every word and feel your enthusiasm.

Where Have You Gone and Where Do You Want to Go?

Here you sit, not enslaved, not beaten on a daily basis, and yet you can't figure out why you have this sinking feeling in your gut that you picked a profession you either hate, or simply don't really understand. Perhaps you are at that critical juncture, the fifth year—the year in which only two-thirds continue on in the profession while one-third drop out. This is where having created that plan, giving yourself a track to run on, can pull you out of the doldrums and back into the realm of enthusiastic educator.

Your plan was filled with measurable benchmarks to determine the answer to this question and to move on. Look at that plan. Review your successes and pat yourself on the back. You have created realistic short- and long-range plans because of the thoroughness of your reconnaissance. You opened the year with the look and demeanor of a professional. You communicated your rules and established your authority early. You attended some helpful seminars to add to your teaching skills. You built a great support network both with the teachers and outside professionals. By looking at each of these elements used in teaching and public speaking, you can tell where you've been, and only then can you even begin to think about your future.

THE PROBLEM I have attended every available teaching seminar. I have applied their ideas, and I have seen some of the great responses from some students. I still know I'm not getting to all of my students, and can't figure out if I have really gotten any better at either teaching or time management.

THE SOLUTION It sounds like you need some serious reflection time. If it can wait until summer break, go away at that time. If you can't afford to go to the seashore to let the sound of the ocean wash through the cobwebs building in your mind, get a wave sound machine for your bedroom, and some nicely scented candles. Try getting a full-body massage. The idea is to relax your mind so you can stand back and take that long look. Then, when thoroughly relaxed, take out your five-year plan and analyze it year by year and semester by semester. If you haven't arrived at the conclusion that you have been making steady progress, or even that your progress has occurred by leaps followed by seemingly nothing, you should consider changing professions. From what you have said, you will find that you are a concerned, educated professional, and the children in your school benefit from your teaching.

Look At Your Rules and Their Purposes

Did you violate any of your rules, and, if so, how often? Did any of your rules cause a reduction in the number of students who stayed in your school? Did any rule that you created and the principal then foisted upon all the other teachers in your school create more turnover, both among the teaching staff and the maintenance crew? Did your students' SAT or ACT scores improve? How do the number of confrontations involving your rules compare this year to prior years? If the number is not declining, you need to find out why.

The real purpose for your rules is to maintain the proper decorum so as to allow you to teach the way you know you must. Have any rules actually run counter to that purpose? If you set a rule out of spite, it will bite you where you can't reach, and may have done so by now.

Your Continuing Education and Professional Development

Becoming a professional only begins with acquiring knowledge and finishing a level of study that qualifies you to receive payment for the exercise of that knowledge. Professionalism, however, means having the qualities or characteristics of a profession or a professional person.

Let's not get hung up in semantics. You know that people pay you for teaching something to others. If you keep that definition in mind, and also never forget that time and people and societies change and so must you, then you're on the right track.

You will receive something in the mail almost every day from a firm or person purporting to have a new twist or book that will improve your teaching skills. How do you know which ones to choose? Should you just ignore all of them and wait for your principal to send you somewhere for further training? Waiting for your principal or anyone to handle your career will take care of your career for you. Unfortunately, you may not like the result.

When all these various offers show up, ask your fellow teachers what they think. Especially ask the teachers you respect for staying on top of their game. Take a look from time to time at the Internet education sources. Go to *www.google.com* and enter search terms such as "English teachers seminars," "math teachers seminars," "science teachers seminars," "social studies seminars," "music teachers seminars," "Web design seminars," "elementary teachers seminars," and so on.

Always stay in contact with your college, and also the local colleges if you have moved away from where your college is located. Look into graduate studies programs. Not only will having a graduate degree enhance your teaching skills, but most schools pay more for it.

Finally, most school systems require continuing your education whether it results in a higher degree or not. A part and parcel of teaching is maintaining current teaching knowledge. Besides, learning more will provide more ideas and invigorate your classroom style. You don't want to become stale. After all, how do you know that you won't discover a better way to motivate or discipline or lecture if you don't explore?

THE PROBLEM I get all kinds of advertisements on education seminars, books, magazines, and online programs. I don't have the time to check into each one.

THE SOLUTION This is another time management issue. When you are looking over your mail to sort it and file it, set up a file for educational programs. Unless the one you just picked up really catches your eye (maybe meaning a good advertising agent and not necessarily a good program), file them. When you are taking that closer look every other week or at some predetermined regular interval, take out the ones that look at all interesting. Post them on the bulletin board in the teacher's lounge along with a note on a full-sized sheet of paper asking if anyone has ever gone to a seminar put on by that source or those sources. Ask for comments on the sheet. No comments, or negative comments, means drop the ad in the circular file.

The Classroom of the Future

Now comes the fun part of writing this book. What can be more interesting or exciting for a teacher trying to help other teachers than to prognosticate on what a classroom will look like in the next generation? Let's begin by looking back a few generations into the history of the public school system.

Do you think Horace Mann would be amazed at where public education is today? His vision with the Lyceums in the nineteenth century was to simply offer speakers to the common man so that not only the rich had access to expanding their knowledge as had been the case historically. Because of Mann the nineteenth century, with those meetings, had witnessed the meager beginnings of the local public school systems we have today. Characterized by the frugality and simplicity of our largely rural agricultural economy, with little in the way of public funds, the classic one-room schoolhouse stood proud.

The school day often began with each student bringing a lump of coal for the potbellied stove to warm them while the teacher, often with only the equivalent of what we recognize today as a high school education, read out loud from the sole textbook. The school year was designed around the farm work so the students could be available to their family for plowing, planting, and harvesting the crops.

Teaching consisted mainly of literacy, penmanship, and good manners. Memorization and recitation were the only means of testing, since the school supplies only consisted of one small blackboard, some chalk, and the desks made by the parents of the children. There was also generally a barn nearby where the children could house their horses while in school. The barn needed maintaining, and the horses needed tending and feeding. The families all helped by performing these tasks, because getting an education was a very important part of growing up. The twentieth century saw the educational systems taken over by the state and local governments as the communities and their needs grew, along with their wealth. By the end of that century and the beginning of the twenty-first century, the country began to experience the problems of aging school buildings as well as a society with educational needs seeming to grow faster than the systems could evolve. The changes in the society from the simple agrarian of two hundred years before had become a huge challenge for the educators. Inner city poverty and the use of illegal drugs and increasing crime within the educational community of children added to the enormity of the challenge. And that brings us to today.

If we look at the technological changes that have taken place just within the last two generations we see the advent of the calculator, the computer, the personal computer, the laptop, the cell phone, the interactive electronic whiteboards, and the distance-learning capabilities. One can only imagine that keeping up with future changes may well be the greatest challenge educators will face, because human beings are social creatures. They want and need human companionship, something none of these technologies engages.

I suggest with a high degree of certainty that the next generation will see education taking place without need of the buildings we use today, except for housing some form of communication equipment. After all, today you can graduate from some colleges without setting foot on their campus, taking all your classes online. It's only a matter of time until you can do that for high school and elementary education. Miniaturization of computer components will continue the reduction in the size of computers until everyone can easily transport them in a pocket or small purse. Then distance learning will have no limit, as the student will be able to carry a pocket-sized, magnificently powerful computer/telephone/ television that will display images on any flat surface.

Energy is not likely to become less expensive, and that will become the driving force for the near elimination of the combustion engine. Individualized transportation will reduce to pleasure trips only.

The down side of all these changes is that we social creatures will begin to lose our natural empathy for our fellow man without the social intercourse that supports it. Loss of that empathy will mean more impersonal means of providing health care, with the needs of science taking precedence over the human need to feel well, live happily, and be treated humanely. I believe it inevitable that the educational system will follow those social trends, and that by the end of this century there will be no classroom to manage unless we elevate the human needs over the technological. And that will take monumental effort by you, the classroom teacher.

Your next assignment even while performing your daily profession of teaching should be to take a serious look at your current social support systems of places like the church halls, city halls, senior centers, facilities for athletic events, etc. These may be the first places that the children will gather for learning the social skills they now get in the structured environment of our schools.

Stay prepared.

References

Alexander, Max. May 2006. Ahead of the Curve. *Reader's Digest* Special Issue.

Krzyzewski, Mike, and Donald T. Phillips. 2000. *Leading with the Heart.* New York: Warner Books.

McGraw, Phillip C. 2001. *Self Matters.* New York: Simon & Schuster Source.

North Central Commission on Accreditation and School Improvement. *Raising Student Achievement: Practices that Work.* 4-4 March 2006. www.ncacasi.org/publications/eseries/

Peale, Norman Vincent. 1961. *The Tough-Minded Optimist.* Englewood Cliffs, NJ: Prentice-Hall.

Wootan, Fred C. 1993. *The Successful Insurance Agency.* Dayton, OH: Atlantic Digital Pub.

Sources Cited

A step towards the creation of educational technology standards: Identifying key skills. Retrieved from www .teach-nology.com/tutorials/tech_standards1/print.htm.

Elson, John. 1978. Pedagogical Incompetence and the Courts. *Theory into Practice* 17 (4), The Schools and the Courts: 303–313.

Franks, Tommy. *American Soldier.* 2004. New York: Regan Books.

Gemelli, Ralph. 1996. *Normal Child and Adolescent Development.* Washington, DC: American Psychiatric Press.

Individuals with Disabilities Education Improvement Act of 2004 (IDEA). www.ed.gov/policy/special/guid/idea2004 .html.

Kohn, Alfie. 1996. *Beyond Discipline: From Compliance to Community.* Alexandria, VA: Association for Supervision and Curriculum Development.

Kottler, Ellen, Jeffrey A. Kottler, and Cary J. Kottler. 1998. *Secrets for Secondary School Teachers.* Thousand Oaks, CA: Corwin Press.

Lawlis, Frank. 2004. *The ADD Answer: How to Help Your Child Now.* New York: Viking.

McDougall, W. 1926. The Growth of Self-Consciousness and of the Self-Regarding Sentiment. In *An Introduction to Social Psychology,* 179–214. Boston: John W. Luce Co.

North Central Commission on Accreditation and School Improvement. Raising student achievement: Practices that work. March 2006. www.ncacasi.org.

Stevenson, Kenneth R. 2002. Ten educational trends shaping school planning and design. Washington, DC: National Clearinghouse for Educational Facilities.

National Assessment of Education Progress. The Nation's Report Card NAEP Trends in Academic Progress Washington, D.C. www.ed.gov/programs/naep/index.html

National Center for Educational Statistics Long-Term Trend Youth Indicators, 2005 within the U.S. Department of Education. http://nces.ed.gov/programs/youthindicators/Indicators.asp?PubPageNumber=2&Show/Tab/. 2005

United States Department of Education. Report on the Study on School Violence and Prevention. Document #2001-037, www.ed.gov/offices/ous/PES/studies-school-violence/3-exec-sum.pdf.

Wooden, John, with Jack Tobin. 2004. *They Call Me Coach*. Chicago: Contemporary Books.

Overview of Education and Enrollment Trends

Do not let the headlines about crime in our schools dictate your classroom management style. The United States Department of Education national studies indicate that students away from school suffer from three (3) times the number of violent crimes as students in school. Homicide also rarely occurs in schools. Theft and fighting without weapons make up the preponderance of crime as reported by schools. (Report on School Violence and Prevention) Some schools have a higher incidence of crime because they are located in violent crime areas, which are not necessarily in the central cities. And crime is not what this is all about anyway. Yes, it has become a factor in certain areas, but, overall, it has not deterred educators from the task at hand.

You must consider the grade level of student education, and the academic progress when taking a look at the overall national educational picture. While the high school completion rate has remained static at 85 percent since 1976, the percentage of twenty-five to twenty-nine-year-olds who received a high school diploma or equivalency certificate has increased eight percent since 1971, and 57 percent of these young adults received additional education. This upward trend leads us to believe that there has been an overall increase in high school graduates who enroll in college immediately following graduation from high school. The percentage of twenty-five to twenty-nine-year-olds who received a bachelor's degree or higher increased from some 17 percent in 1971 to 29 percent in 2005. Unfortunately, the percentage differences between whites and blacks and between whites and Hispanics have increased, which portends a wider economic gulf later in their lives.

Academically, if we look back over the history of that same thirty-year period, we find that on average, nine-year-olds scored higher in reading and mathematics in 2004 than any previous year. Thirteen-year-olds scored higher in math than in any previous year. Seventeen-year-olds also scored higher in math in 2004, and the white/black score gap became smaller. One caveat we have to keep in mind when looking at the long-term trend and main assessment programs is that they are not comparable: students were sampled by age for the long-term trend assessments and by grade for the main assessments. Therefore, there are no achievement levels in the long-term trend, as there are in the main assessment. Also we found that the long-term trend results were available at the national level, while the main National Assessment of Education Progress (NAEP) has results at the state and large-district level in some states. (United States Department of Education National Center of Educational Statistics Long Term Trend Youth Indicators 2005)

The "academic report describes long-term trends in nine-, thirteen-, and nineteen-year-olds' achievement in reading and mathematics during the last three decades." (United States)

This report is not a statement of the quality or effectiveness of America's educational system, but simply a reporting of the results. It appears that the average reading scores for nine-year-olds was up approximately 5 percent in 2004 as compared to 1971; the scores for thirteen-year-olds in that period were up less than 2 percent; and the scores for seventeen-year-olds had no statistically significant change for the same period.

The mathematics report was based on test results of students aged nine, thirteen, and seventeen. It assessed the students' knowledge of basic facts, their ability to carry out numerical operations using only paper and pencil, and their knowledge of basic formulas for geometry. The average mathematics scores for nine- and thirteen-year-olds was up approximately 10 percent, or twenty-two points, while the change in scores of the seventeen-year-olds was statistically insignificant.

You could say that our elementary schools have done a better job than the high schools but, before reaching that conclusion, we must look at the changes in the student population over that same period. There has been no increase in the proportion of African-American children, but an increase of 18 percent in the proportion of Hispanic students. Due to the high dropout rate within the black community and the difficulty that the Hispanic students often have with the English language, those dropouts and Hispanic language difficulties have actually acted to smooth out and even lessen these changes from 1971 until 2005. This trend for an increase in the percentage of Hispanics compared to white children is expected to continue and even increase. By the year 2020 the white non-Hispanic population is expected to decrease by 2.4 percent, the black population to increase by 3.5 percent, the Hispanic to increase by 18.9 percent, and the Asian/other Pacific Islanders to increase by 18.8 percent. You see, then, that the mix within the school-age population will continue to change significantly over the next thirteen years.

There is also the current trend away from large public schools where one size fits all, and identical buildings mean equal quality of education, and toward magnet schools, giving parents a choice of where to send their children. However, there is no data supporting the idea that smaller, magnet schools are better or will increase graduation rates, and it may well turn out that the smaller school concept is too expensive for the public sector (Stevenson, 2002).

The next trend is consistent with the smaller building concept; it is a trend toward smaller numbers of students in the classrooms, meaning reduced student/teacher ratios. This concept is supported by the introduction of many distance-learning capabilities and technologies used within the school buildings themselves, such as closed circuit television, which allow one teacher to teach more students at any one time yet have fewer in the classroom. Children who are having a hard time passing mandatory math tests may be required to take remedial math courses and forgo taking arts courses or music, or even vocational courses, thereby causing a trend toward the basic courses of reading, writing, and math.

Children may spend more time in school in order to gain the abilities necessary to pass the state-required tests, thereby potentially increasing the average number of days in school from the present 180 to 240 days in a year. Paper use as we know it will diminish in favor of digital communications. Some school districts are already moving toward providing K–12 all under one roof, which sounds as if we will have come full circle back to the one-room schoolhouse of the nineteenth century. However, the students will not really be handled the same way they were then. Finally, schools as we know them will end before the end of the twenty-first century (Stevenson, 2002).

Near-term trends in enrollment reflect rapid growth at the elementary level, spilling into the high school level in one to eight years and will continue even beyond this because of the rapid Hispanic migration to the United States. However, it is my belief that toward the end of this century, as technological advances meet the challenges of these increased enrollments, the need for facilities will diminish but the need for qualified teachers will continue to grow.

INDEX

About the Author

FREDERICK C. WOOTAN, an award winning poetry author, entered teaching three years ago after thirty successful years in the insurance business. During those years he created, wrote and taught many continuing education insurance courses for insurance agents. He has written several articles for nationally published trade magazines, two mystery novels, one textbook on insurance, and one inspirational book for teens that is mandatory outside reading for the juniors at Bishop Fenwick High School where he teaches. His experience as a manager brought a different perspective to the teaching field. He resides with his wife in Waynesville, Ohio.

About the Foreword Writer and Technical Reviewer

CATHERINE H. MULLIGAN, a teacher, department chairman, dean of academics, and now principal at Bishop Fenwick High School. She not only has taught at the high school level but taught at the college level for over thirty years. She has received many awards for her teaching, community service, as well as study from the Woodrow Wilson National Fellowship Foundation Institute, Princeton University, during the summer of 1989. She served as Master Teacher in the Torch outreach program of the Woodrow Wilson Foundation, and published articles in mathematics magazines for teachers. She resides with her husband in Middletown, Ohio.